The Fallacy
of Wildlife
Conservation

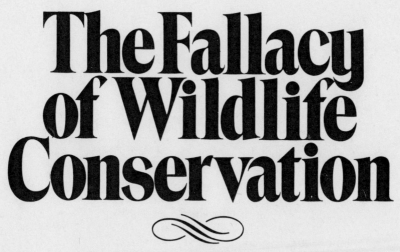

The Fallacy of Wildlife Conservation

by John A. Livingston

McCLELLAND AND STEWART

Reprinted 1982

McClelland and Stewart Limited
The Canadian Publishers
25 Hollinger Road
Toronto Ontario
M4B 3G2

Some of these thoughts have appeared in different form in presentations, some of them subsequently published, to the Algonquin Wildlands League, the Canadian Association of Landscape Architects, the Canadian Federation of Humane Societies, the Federal-Provincial Wildlife Conference, the Federation of Ontario Naturalists, and the Soil Conservation Society of America.

Canadian Cataloguing in Publication Data

Livingston, John A., 1923-
    The fallacy of wildlife conservation

ISBN 0-7710-5335-5 (bound)
ISBN 0-7710-5336-3 (pbk.)

1. Wildlife conservation. I. Title.

QL82.L58   333.95   C80-094817-3

Printed and bound in the United States of America

Contents

ACKNOWLEDGEMENTS

I wrote the first draft of this in Baja California Sur, Mexico, and Kuantan, Malaysia, while on sabbatical leave from the Faculty of Environmental Studies, York University. I thank my former graduate student, Ursula Jolin, whose logic is inspired and whose questioning is merciless.

John A. Livingston
Sunderland, Ontario
1980

NOTE TO THE READER

Although the preservation of wildlife is both my bias and my vehicle, this essay is really about the difference between living and being, which is sometimes called "quality of life." It was written in response to a direct challenge. For years I had been uncritically mouthing the conservation catechism; it was time to think it through. What follows is an account of that process.

CHAPTER ONE
The Background

I am not a biologist, an ecologist, nor indeed an "ologist" of any kind. I am merely a naturalist, for whom logic and "the word" have come to count for little. Nature, praise be, neither talks nor is rational, and therein is comfort.

Naturalists become accustomed to travelling light but, still, there are the accumulated impedimenta of a lifetime; in a little pouch of talismans I carry such things as the scent of fresh tiger dung in the monsoon jungle and the stench of two million puffins on fogged St. Kilda. There is the loving rasp of tundra saxifrage across my palm and the shocking sear of man-of-war tentacles around my chest. I once ate a malarial mosquito distended with my blood and I can summon up the after taste of fried musk-ox cheek. My bones have felt a hyena I could not see, crushing a wildebeest skull, and I have celebrated, with a cock peafowl, crowing in the night. Odours, touches, tastes, sounds – all part of what at this moment is me. This is not to say that I have not *seen* much – I have – but one learns that visual traces can game at chance with the memory; not only are pictures illusory, but also seeing is believing, and believing can be a one-way street.

I am a conservationist, a nature preservationist, and I have smelled the exhausts and the people and their works, heard the slogans and the guns and the exhortations, felt the nylon and the concrete, tasted the saccharin and the tenderizer. I no longer dare to *look*. The last time I looked, there was an endless tumbling cataract of identical managers, administrators, and technicians. There wasn't a freedman in sight. There were a few splashes of pigeon whitewash on a massive bunker that houses an institution of higher training and, within it, coveys of tight-lipped souls with pocket calculators and hard briefcases bent on "managing our world's resources for the future" through rational planning, design, and development. Next time, *you* look, I'm busy ruminating.

A ruminant is a cud-chewer—a cow or a goat. To extract optimum nourishment, the ruminant chews and swallows its fodder, then brings it up later for further chewing at leisure. The human ruminant, as exemplified by the videotape highlight analyst or the academic, is a re-hasher. As it is for the hoofed being, re-hashing for the human being can be a highly beneficial exercise. In light of our peculiar human specialization, perhaps for "re-hash" we should read "re-view." In this essay I want to review a few things about wildlife and conservation and some related matters.

One way or another, I have been involved in wildlife conservation all of my adult and a good portion of my sub-adult life. It follows, if only by definition, that I have known frustration deeply and long. There are all manner of frustrations in conservation, of which one of the more obvious would be that which arises after you have laboured long and assiduously in the vineyard only to have somebody fly along and dump herbicide all over it. But most of our problems are subtler.

No abrasion stings more than that which is caused by one's own carelessness, stupidity, or indeed innocence. No bruise is more tender than that which is one's own fault. Indeed, perhaps no resentment is deeper than that of which the source is directly traceable to oneself. We in the wildlife conservation cabal have enjoyed a few successes, but failure and futility have become our familiars, and we are hurting. Our overwhelming losses can instantly, easily, be attributed to the urban-industrial process of scarification, to world human populations, to institutional greeds, and all the rest of it. But such excuses are much too facile. To lay the total blame here, I feel, is a species of Afghanistanism: railing and shaking your fist at an unseen foe who is quite unaware of your existence, much less your fury. Better to stay closer to home. The fault is not and never was "out there."

Not that we have not worked and thought hard; we have. It is true that we have always lacked the financial muscle to play the political game where that game is played, and that we have lacked the ideological empathy of the majority of the "general public," but these are no more than the facts of our existence. Disadvantage is simply the environment of conservation; it always will be. But there are many admirable beings who prosper in apparently wholly inhospitable surroundings. See a baby Lapland longspur crack its natal shell warm and pulsing in a June arctic blizzard; see a yellow wood sorrel crack asphalt; see a gosling or a turtle hatchling leg it across the sand to the sea amidst a flurry of gulls or frigate-birds. Our "hostile" environment is slim excuse.

I think that a depressingly large portion of the wildlife conservation effort has been entirely wasted. In view of the fact that in the conservation energy budget there is no margin for waste, no subcutaneous fat for emergencies, this is all the more alarming. If I am even partially right, then it might be well to review our ineffectiveness, to isolate even a few of the more obvious contributing factors. I think this is a worthwhile exercise. We have nothing to lose.

Defensive action – delaying action – is always terribly busy and reflexive and reactive, simply because there usually is not time in which to regroup, dig in, consider, and strategise. Confusion and fragmentation – and exhausting flailing – often follow. Such would be my characterization of wildlife conservation: we dart about, stamping at tiny smoulders in the carpet, rushing from hot spot to hot spot, when all the while the roof is racing to a fire-storm and the walls are creaking toward collapse.

People in the "line" of conservation fire-fighting (there is nothing you could call "staff") have rarely had time to draw back and take a painstaking look at what we are actually doing. Each of us no doubt waxes choleric over both the priorities and the pathetically limited ranges of action of the organizations we support, and each of us has a personal short list of critical hot spots. Which will it be – polar bear, Kirtland's warbler, clouded leopard, fin whale, tuatara, Sumatran rhino? But I am not going to get into that. I want to speak in more general terms about some questions that very rarely make it even to the absolute bottom of the agenda. Some practising conservationists may not want to hear about them at all; for a long time I did not. Now I find them inescapable.

I suspect that our difficulties may be more entrenched and obstinate than many of the more "activist" among us appear to realize. It is one thing to raise placards in the street and another to put the aggregate messages to content analysis. That is what I will try to do here. No doubt many will see this as the most reprehensible cop-out – avoidance of action. At a younger age, I was repeatedly instructed by John H. Baker, the late distinguished president of the National Audubon Society, to keep my shirt on, for the love of God. I choose to believe now that if we sit down, catch our breath, wipe our spectacles, and walk – not run – back to the mêlée, we may yet extend the day.

In the course of this pause for reflection, I want to address not the practice but the *argument* for wildlife conservation. Of course there is no single argument – they are many and varied – but all involve reason and logic of one sort or another. I want to look at that reasoning process. In conservation we have always assumed a dialogue between ourselves and everyone else; a civilized, adversary proceeding in which reason, logic, and meticulous argument, liberally laced with horrible precedent, would persuade just men and women to our position. We have invested enormously in that assumption. Unfortunately for reason and logic, for ourselves, and for wildlife, it has not worked. One would like to know why.

What follows cannot be exhaustive. I do not pretend to know all of the factors that are involved. I shall stick to those with which I have had some experience. Suspecting as I do, however, that we have been effectively arguing *against* ourselves, in the first part of this essay I shall look at some of the "stock" or "set-piece" arguments, and try to weigh their utility and identify some of their implications. Then I shall try to abstract some of the more deeply imbedded malignancies that, perversely enough, seem to thrive and prosper on our arguments much as forest, field, and garden "pests" respond to biocides. Finally I wish to speculate—admittedly in a very personal way—on possible alternatives or at least on supplemental ways and means.

This search is important for several reasons. After spending more years than I really care to count in trying to advocate the *practice* of wildlife conservation—the "doing"—I became interested in trying to understand the fundamental *notion* of wildlife conservation—the "knowing." Wildlife conservation not necessarily as an activity, but as a state of mind. Because it is always so easy to set down in little square boxes someone *else's* motives, and to impute and attribute and assign perceptions and beliefs to others, much thought was then invested in describing the peculiar state of mind of the opposition (still assuming an adversary proceeding).

I have written and lectured on the historical and cultural roots of a state of mind pervasive in the western world (but not unique to it) that appears to be implacably indifferent to wild nature. The western cosmology would appear to be so firmly man-centred that the very notion of wildlife conservation can barely be entertained in any profound sense. Much of the conservationist's frustration arises when, even though his argument appears to be apprehended intellectually, it is obvious at the same time that the emotional or spiritual shift from the cool abstract to the hot-flowing, pumping urgency of *living* is for some reason impossible. It is as though the necessary "leap" into our own biological context cannot even be conceived, much less entertained.

But even abstract intellectual grasp of the argument is rarely achieved. There are few experiences quite so cruel as, when after having made a well-argued, even elegant and moving case to someone, you lean back expecting the warm sparkle of shared insight and understanding, only to encounter the flat opaqueness of complete and utter incomprehension. The lecturer whose delightedly prepared joke flops wetly flat knows how the wildlife conservationist feels.

As anyone who professes for a living has to learn sooner or later, if one's little academic jests develop a consistent pattern of failure, then perhaps it might not be wise to invest too much energy in sifting for faults in one's audience, but rather in going over one's own material. That is why I have set about trying to understand our own array of arguments for conservation and to assess, as best I can, their effectiveness and worth, their actual result. That is not easy. Anyone undertaking such a task, whether stand-up comedian, evangelist, or soothsayer, knows that cleaning up one's act can be an untidy and often painful process. I have as deep an emotional and practical investment in this question as any reader, and what follows may not always be flattering. But again, we have very little to lose. Just as I write this, a new modulation in the song of a magpie-robin outside tells me we may have something to gain.

Like it or not, we shall first have to deal with definitions. Such a procedure can often be dull, but in this case it is vital. One reason is that the words "conservation," "ecology," and "environment" have been so widely and so cynically co-opted in our time that they barely retain a shred of their original meanings. Another reason is that I am weary of playing semantical games of the jesuitical sort so adored by the humanists, who are no longer biological beings, but of some other cosmic stuff. This is simply to say that the ground rules here are going to be those of wildlife preservation.

Very generally, by convention, "conservation" has meant the care of "natural resources" and their protection from depletion, waste, and damage, so that they will be readily at hand through perpetuity. Traditionally we have used this approach for soil, water, vegetation, and, in a more particular way, to those kinds of animals (fishes, fur-bearing mammals, waterfowl, and the like) in which there is a commercial or other special interest. More recently we have begun to see "sustainability" in some endangered plant and animal species and associations. For these, the long-term goal is not necessarily exploitation, but rather preservation in the cause of what are considered to be somewhat higher human aspirations and values than sheer consumption. In fact, the more recent and interesting of the wildlife conservation arguments tend to coalesce around these latter aspirations and values, but in order to understand their genesis and evolution, and their implications, we must review those justifications for conservation that many of us might consider more crass.

(Quite recently, you will have noticed an increasing tendency to separate out and indeed to polarize "conservation" and "preservation." Many hunters, developers, planners, managers, and others will proclaim themselves as being conservation-oriented in the most modern, aware, and realistic way, by contrast with the old-fashioned, stubborn "preservationists" who squat sullenly and stupidly in the way of orderly progress. This peculiar conceptual dichotomy is obviously as useful to the production-consumption parade as it is destructive of wild nature. Preservation smells of reaction, retrogression, primitivism, and worse, while environmental assessment, regional planning, ecological development, and all the other appurtenances of the techno-machine are permitted, through "conservation," to assume their proper heroic roles.)

Traditionally, "resources" (including wildlife) have been perceived in an entirely utilitarian light. Someone has observed insightfully that resources do not exist in and of themselves; they *become*. The moment we see usefulness in something – any-thing – that thing becomes a resource. Resources are human assets. Natural resources are those assets that were put in place by natural processes, such as trees or uranium, and that we can draw upon as required, for such purposes as the extractor (and by extension, society) sees fit.

We have drawn a distinction between "renewable" resources and those, particularly minerals, that are "nonrenewable"; once you take them out of the ground you cannot replace them, or grow more of them. At one time, this seemed a reasonable approach, but in our own day it may become difficult to maintain. More on that later.

By definition, a "resource" of any kind has *intrinsic utility*. If we could not use it, then it would not be a resource. This applies equally to "renewables" and "nonrenewables," including wildlife. The notion of *use* is central and nuclear. At one point we began to make a further distinction, in this case between "consumptive" and "nonconsumptive" uses of renewable resources, including wildlife. Consumptive uses of wildlife would be fishing, sealing, whaling, sport hunting, and the like, in which the individual being is "consumed" (killed). We cannot use it without killing it. Whether we literally consume (eat) the animal is irrelevant here; we have taken it out of circulation for good. In contrast to this, we have such "nonconsumptive" uses of wildlife as birdwatching, nature photography, or skindiving, in which, although we *use* animals, we do not kill them. This once-useful distinction has also become blurred.

But we see in wildlife and other "resources" more than utility. Just as important, perhaps more so, is the unstated but implicit assumption that the use, whatever it is, is vested solely and exclusively in the human interest. The ownership and the proprietorship are ours alone. The balance sheet is the human balance sheet, and assets whether current or fixed are man's inalienable property. Thus man has private ownership of and vested interest in diamonds and anchovies, topsoil and snow geese, duckweed, balsawood, and sperm whales. Human beings have absolute, divinely conferred right of access to these "resources" for whatever human uses may be contrived. The fundamental concept of "resource" is clear and unequivocal.

So it is that when we draft a conservation rationale, almost without exception, we argue the case in terms of the human interest. It does not matter which of our several constituencies we may be addressing. At the simplest level there are identifiable special interests in agriculture, forestry, fisheries, mining, recreational fishing, and shooting. These are obvious. Also we have the special interest of science and technology: clearly we have an investment in the preservation of the raw material of knowledge, with all of its implications for research, education, technical application, and so on – the advancement of human affairs in general. Finally we have the apparently growing body of people who have an interest in the preservation of nature for aesthetic, ethical, or even spiritual reasons. But even this interest is no less "vested," in the sense of implicit payoff. There is a future benefit to us.

The definition of "wildlife conservation" that I use daily, and from which I am working here, is this:

> The preservation of wildlife forms and groups of forms in perpetuity, for their own sakes, irrespective of any connotation of present or future human use.

By "wildlife forms and groups of forms" I mean living beings and groups of living beings (associations) existing in a natural state:

plants, animals, and their habitats. I explicitly exclude from this definition: man and other domestic and feral animals and plants; species introduced by man and living in foreign environments; and man-dependent species. This last means that as long as there are people around, there is no need to expend any effort preserving rats and silverfish. In essence, wildlife conservation is the preservation of nonhuman beings in their natural settings, unaffected by human influence or activity, uncontaminated by human antibiosis, emancipated from human serfdom.

I hasten to acknowledge that there are few places on planet Earth that are not at least indirectly touched by man and his accomplishments. I am very much aware that besides being idealistic, my definition has the usual taint of proprietorship – or at the very least, paternalism – that seems to characterize most of our attitudes (intellectual-emotional positions) with respect to nonhuman nature. I trust you will forgive me, on the grounds that each of us, more is the pity, is no more than human and we must communicate in human terms; that there would be no need for "conservation" – itself a wholly human concept and activity – were there no human creature; and that we ourselves created the vacuum into which the need for conservation flows, and nobody else is going to do anything about it.

Whatever your individual perception or definition of what wildlife conservation is, or might be, our collective track record is spelled out in nauseating detail in many a readily available place; I am not going to recount it here. Most historical accounts of conservation activities tend to arise from the special perspective of whoever happened to write those accounts, and thus are just as biased as my perceptions and yours. There are many perspectives; take your choice. If you happen to be interested in the captive rearing of birds, you will have been much rewarded by the resurrection of the Hawaiian goose, and you will be watching the current breeding programs for whooping cranes and peregrines. If you happen to be a duck-shooter you will be able to point to the many habitat-restoration programs your organizations have undertaken. (If you were to take a slightly closer look, you might see that you have not left enough ducks to fill the habitat available to them.)

If your interest is endangered species in general you will be watching efforts toward specific reserves and legislative controls of exploitation and destruction. (If *you* look harder, you will see that the 'ologists and legislators cannot yet decide what an endangered species *is*!) If you are a park or zoo enthusiast you will have noticed the recent proliferation of both. If you are an ethologist you will be pleased by recent spectacular advances in your science, this time among wild animals. If you are a television viewer you will have come to know an endless assortment of "nature-adventure" programs. On the other hand, if you are that unidentifiable "impartial man-in-the-street," you may very well have become a little jaded by the omnipresent multichannel trumpetings of "environmentalism," which whatever it is should not be confused with wildlife preservation.

Whoever you are, whatever your special or even peripheral interest, it is very difficult to back away from immediate specifics for a wider-angle view. Each of us who has the remotest concern for wildlife is at least a kind of specialist. Each of us has places, landscapes, species, habitats, problems, that especially preoccupy us. Each of us is cranky about *something* a little more than the rest. I happen to like the desert, the tropical forest, and the arctic more than most other places; I loathe cities and love the sea; I prefer predators to herbivores; I like birds of any size more than small mammals; I prefer non-game to game species; I am pleased about symbiosis and bored by taxonomy. I like mysteries. There is no profound significance in any of this; it is merely the way I am. The way each of us is, the way each of us sees, and feels, and responds.

So when I invite you to join me in zooming back a little for a broader perspective on wildlife conservation I do so in full awareness of the bias that shapes and directs my own reflections. Nevertheless, I think that I should make the effort. And if I can, you can. When you do, I am certain that you will come to the same conclusion: in the broadest sense, wildlife preservation is a catastrophic, heart-breaking disaster.

The dismal figures are widely published and well-known. The terrifying trends are readily visible. I will not detail any of it here save to remind you that the torpedoed Ark is settling with all hands – varieties, races, populations, species, associations, communities, whole faunas – and almost without a sound.

Remember that as the absolute number of organisms, species, and groups of species diminishes, the likelihood of recovery is geometrically rather than arithmetically reduced. Also, since the crucible out of which these vanishing miracles were formed is *all of Earth time*, and the devastation has taken place in no more than a wink of *human* time, things are in no position to take care of themselves. The wonderful mutualistic, compliant, selfless, all-encompassing orchestration of relationships which is in process of brutal eradication can never be reformed, rebuilt, reassembled, "restructured." By comparison with the biosphere, Humpty-Dumpty is child's play.

Entirely out of control, the human technomachine guzzles and lurches and vomits and rips its random crazy course over the face of the once-blue planet, as though some filthy barbaric fist were drunkenly swiping with a gigantic paint roller across an ancient tapestry. Unevenness in the rich textured nap of Earth's surface causes the paint to cling slightly unevenly, with scattered spots and holes showing in the roller's wake. These are the success stories. Isolated and discrete as they are, it is quite possible that they can never recombine into a coherent whole.

We are left with a miscellaneous rag-tag assortment of odd and disconnected relics – some larger, some smaller. In general, these gaps or anomalies tend to be in "frontier" regions (arctic, rain-forest), or in the great biological near-desert that is the open ocean. But the mindless machine has long since outgrown all restraint; the paint roller's antibiotic lacquer is thick, and fluid. If you watch, you can see its viscous pools widen, as though of their own volition, toward the farthest reaches of life's lovely tapestry.

Wildlife communities are richer, in terms of numbers of species, in equatorial regions than in higher latitudes. The greatest number of endangered species in the world today live in the tropics and sub-tropics. In underprivileged overpopulated countries I see no glimmer of hope for wildlife. It is simply too much to expect, for an entire catalogue of reasons, that the care and maintenance of wildlife could possibly rise on the list of priorities (including accelerated industrial expansion) that exists in the tropics today. We should remember that there is little or no preservation tradition in most such places, in any event, and to think that such a tradition could spring forth fully developed in the face of current events would be to abdicate common sense altogether. The human orgy has exactly one conceivable outcome for those species that are (a) edible, or (b) compete with man for food, or (c) compete with man for space. Perhaps this will change one day, but not soon. In the meantime, losses will have been colossal and extinctions will have been many. Extinctions without replacement – ever.

On the other hand, there are places in the world that are not yet populated toward the point of ignition. There are some spots not yet painted over, not yet obliterated. In spite of their technical grotesqueness, some of the hypermanaged western nations still have options having to do with open space, natural areas, living nonhuman beings. But even there, we have to admit the utter failure of wildlife conservation either as a practice or as an ethos to penetrate the general consciousness. The acceleration of wildlife extermination is remorseless, even in the "civilized" world–perhaps especially there. There is a general almost total failure to grasp the *notion* of wildlife conservation.

Here I mean societies such as the one I live in, where one might expect the cultural environment for the notion to be wholly favourable. Places where the "haves" live. I do not, by the way, mean regions or nations influenced or dominated by French, Italian, Portuguese, or Spanish traditions, which have never been favourable for wildlife or its protection. On the evidence, wildlife seems to hold its own best in "have" cultures deriving from northern Europe, including Britain, poorest in those deriving from southern Europe. The implications of this must surely be obvious to all but the most doggedly unobservant.

The worst prospect for wildlife is in those countries where human population increase is out of control and/or in those that have inherited the "romance" traditions. And political ideologies have nothing whatever to do with it. When you think about this, it dawns that ownership of the means of production and locus of the distribution of profits are entirely irrelevant to wildlife conservation, as long as the goal of human activity is production. Who cares who owns the whaling fleet, the automobile factory, the petrochemical plant, the jet aircraft assembly line? Who cares where the profits go? What earthly difference does it make to wildlife? Certainly it has never made any difference to conservation.

On a world basis, "wildlife conservation" in its fullest and deepest meaning as "preservation" simply does not exist. That is because its fullest and deepest meaning cannot be expressed in a political platform, a computer printout, an official plan, or a research report. You cannot quantify, analyze, show data, and prove it out. It is not like that. For me, wildlife preservation is a wholly permeating life awareness that has become an unconscious part of every thought, attitude, perception. So it is too with others, many of them; but not *that* many. Not enough to matter.

Then one must ask, why *aren't* there more of us? People in the mass can be and are every day persuaded to the most bizarre assortment of freakish, perverse, weird, and convoluted intellectual positions the craziest of minds can concoct. What is the matter with *us*? Certain (as are all the converted) that there is nothing unhinged about our position–that life is manifestly *right* and that the wilful reduction of life is *wrong*, why are we, the unique possessors of THE WORD, so pathetically inept in adding to our number?

No doubt I will be challenged on this point. Much of the conservation rhetoric calls attention to the growing number of people who have become involved, in one way or another, with our "movement." I have done so earlier in this chapter. That the number is growing in an absolute sense I have no doubt, but then so is everything else growing in an absolute sense–all except wildlife. In a relative sense the story is dismal.

When, for example, you state a case for wildlife to any tier of government, you are told there simply is not sufficient mandate for action of the magnitude that is clearly needed. Insufficient mandate means inadequate constituency. One learns to judge politicians on grounds other than their utterances, but in this case they are absolutely right. We wildlifers like to *claim* that there is a constituency–or several of them–for wildlife preservation, but the harsh and unequivocal record shows that we are neither statistically nor politically significant.

There are abundant reasons for our political failure. First, of course, is the fact that in spite of our widely advertised "environmental" awareness, the polis is the human concentration and admits no other participatory interest. Also, the political tenure system is in polar conflict with ecologic realities; life systems take their own deliberate time, for which new promises in new elections cannot wait. Political process and nature preservation are fundamentally antithetical. And, as I have pointed out already, political ideologies are simply not relevant.

But there is more to our cultures than politics, and there are reasons for our failures that are much less obvious. Indeed there are so many of them, so interwoven, intractable, and complex, that one despairs of ever beginning to do an adequate job of sorting them out. That is why, in this instance, I have chosen not to look so much at our "opposition" but rather more at ourselves.

I do not suggest that our arguments are *the* cause of our failure–they obviously are not–but I shall try to show that they may have played a much more important role than many of us may have realized. In any case, to examine one's own logical process can only be salutary.

Methodologists urge us to begin with a parsimony of assumptions. Mine are rather too many to allow a hyperclinical approach, but no matter. By acknowledging those of which I am aware I may at least begin to expose some of the dimensions of the problem. For purposes of what follows, then:

I assume that wildlife preservation is a good thing.

I assume that there is a rational argument for wildlife preservation.

I assume that whatever that argument is, we have not yet used it effectively.

I assume that argument *can* be used effectively, which is the same thing as saying that I assume that reasonable people respond to reasonable argument.

I hypothesize that those arguments we have used have been unequal to the task.

CHAPTER TWO
The Arguments

Self-Interest

If we can't be good, at least we can be prudent. You do not strangle your own support system. If for no other reason than our own welfare, our own selfishness, we should try to entertain at least the possibility of some slight merit in a conservation-oriented approach to living. This is the core of the self-interest group of arguments. You might go so far as to say that if we cannot appreciate the nature and quality of our acts and anticipate at least some of their consequences, then we have no right to describe ourselves as intelligent, or even sane.

In some contexts this approach works. Not many years ago it would have been unthinkable – preposterous – to suggest that people might actually band together to prevent flights of supersonic aircraft over large cities; or stall the building of airports; or haul mercury, lead, and asbestos poisoners into court; or redirect highways, dams, pipelines, and other such narcissistic exercises. But these have been done, and in the name of self-interest.

These of course are not wildlife issues; they are people issues. There is a world of difference. Let us look at some of the ways in which self-interest is expressed in terms of wildlife.

THE "WISE USE" ARGUMENTS
These are the oldest of the lot, and they appear in a number of varieties. It will help if we isolate a few of the more prevalent of these before considering "wise use" as a whole.

Husbandry
If you treat whatever you are using intelligently, you can help to assure its continuing usefulness. This idea has long been basic in the handling of livestock, ground covers, topsoils, and so on.

Good husbandmen have known it forever. They have known that their interests lay in the interest of whatever they were cultivating, whether cattle and crops, or the soils, water, and vegetation that sustain them. You find the best of husbandry, in the pure sense, in the breeding and rearing of domestic animals, where it is both a science and an art. It seems to involve not only meticulous care but also a kind of special insight that is perhaps no more than an indefinable "feeling" in the experienced stockman. A sort of touch that some have, but most of us have not.

The notion of husbandry was extended to natural as opposed to domesticated resources many years ago, and for very good reason: rural people could understand and appreciate its implications. Whether applied to stands of trees, water sources, watershed slopes, or fertile valley bottoms, good husbandry meant care and sensitivity in their treatment. Such was in both the individual and collective interest.

Husbandry of course can properly apply only to something that is under your total control—your herd, your flock, your vineyard. If it is not under your total control you cannot husband it. Nevertheless the notion was eventually applied to certain forms of wildlife—also with good reason. Those wild animals chosen for "husbandry" were those desired either for commerce or for "sport" (which in the present day is a very real form of commerce). By treating the species concerned intelligently, as a good husbandman, you ensure its continuance in your special interest.

Such, essentially, was the rationale for the first closed game seasons, bag limits, and so on. Later, the regulatory style became much more refined, as in minimum sizes for fishes or "males only" for deer. Still later, wise husbandry dictated the repair, maintenance, and even the construction of suitable breeding habitats for most-desired ducks. There appeared fish hatcheries, transplantations of foreign game birds, wild animal farms, all aspects of what later came to be the massive manipulation of the wildlife "resource." An enormous complex of detail emerged: kinds and sizes of nets for commercial fishes, different bag and possession limits for different species of ducks, and so on. All of it "wildlife husbandry," in the interest of the resource user or consumer.

The notion of "wildlife husbandry" is inherently and ridiculously self-contradictory. Animal husbandry's most important element is selective breeding. If wildlife is wild, then it cannot be husbanded. But it sounds good, no doubt. In an apparent attempt to keep the illusion of husbandry alive, those charged with the delivery of wildlife to the consumer (in North America, chiefly provincial and state departments of fur, fish, and game) chose to describe their work as wildlife "management." This was singularly appropriate, as it tended to anticipate the propriety–indeed the sanctity–of the religion of management in the technocratic age.

There are serious implications. Practitioners of wildlife "management" are almost entirely concerned with the uninterrupted production and mass packaging of commercially important species. Indeed, many contemporary wildlife biologists are frustrated that their charge is so rarely extended to those species (meaning the vast majority of species) not commercially desirable. Although there are some efforts, chiefly at the federal levels in Canada and the United States, work on behalf of non-commercial wildlife is relatively minute in both budget and priority allocations.

More significant are the implications of the husbandry argument as addressed to the public. Emphasizing as it does a few desired species to the almost total exclusion of the overwhelmingly greater list of native plants and animals, it suggests that the former *are indeed* the more important species. If it is to these that virtually all of the effort is directed, then clearly that must be an accurate reflection of the proper priorities. How else is an individual ignorant of wildlife to interpret it? Every day of our lives you and I must accept someone else's judgement on everything from television programming to foreign policy because there are supposedly qualified people making decisions for us on the basis of information we do not have. So it is with "wildlife husbandry." The experts know what they are doing; who am I to question it?

But the problem is deeper. Even assuming that the public were to become more sophisticated about wildlife conservation needs, there remains the matter of the assumed fitness and rightness of good husbandry, intelligent treatment, enlightened management. The important assumption, as the argument is drummed into us by both government agencies and private organizations, is that all of wild nature is a herd, a flock, a crop, to be manipulated and controlled in the public, national, and human interest.

Man is total proprietor, manager, and decision-maker with respect to wildlife. This is the clear-cut and unambiguous message of "good husbandry" conservation. Wildlife is yours; yours to manipulate in your own best interest. If you treat it badly or stupidly, only you (not wildlife) will be the loser; if you treat it well, it is yours from which to profit in perpetuity.

Stewardship

There is more involved, as it turns out, than individual and collective management for profit or loss. The true husbandman, almost by definition, is sensitive to the continuity of things. His knowledge, his insight, and his skills are not vested in him once only and to the exclusion of others. He recognizes both an indebtedness to the past and an obligation to the future, if only in respect to the welfare of his science. He sees himself as temporary proprietor of the herd only, having inherited the wisdom and accumulated experience of generations gone, and carrying the responsibility of refining that experience, to the best of his ability, toward its further refinement when his time is over.

This is the good steward personified. He sees himself as no more than short-term custodian, performing an honest and honourable task that in its total scope transcends the individual human lifetime. Thus it is that the appeal for conservation is directed to an entire generation of such custodians. Or, on another plane, it is addressed to all of mankind in respect to the biosphere itself, in the service of a higher spiritual power.

The ultimate stewardship entreaty, which casts man in the role of resident manager on behalf of the Creator, is for many people a reasonably palatable interpretation of Old Testament injunctions having to do with man's "dominion" over nonhuman nature. Taken literally – as they frequently are – the Biblical pronouncements crash and reverberate to the drums and jackboots of absolute tyranny. Interpreted, however, as direction to a kind of benign caretaking, in the name of God, with the resident manager responsible and answerable to God, the instruction becomes tolerable to many people.

Indeed, if for "God" we were to read "life process," or "biosphere," or "cosmic continuity," or some such, there would seem to be relatively few of us who could not act comfortably within this stricture. That it does effectively confer absolute power and authority – if only temporarily – on the custodian is not seen by most as too grave a problem because with that power and authority go responsibility and answerability. Clearly nothing could be in the better interest of the temporary custodian than to do his job wisely and well. In this way the good husbandman is serving an even higher interest than the human collective in the here and now, and even in the future.

This refinement of the "husbandry" argument is similar with respect to the seat of power and authority in the relationship between man and the rest of nature. Even though we are in the divine service, on Earth we are unquestionably in charge. If we treat resources badly or stupidly, we are not only the losers in the sense of our continuing vested interest, but also we have violated a divine charge. If we treat them well, not only is our tangible reward on Earth immediate and bountiful, but also we may expect the subsequent benefits due to loyal and faithful servants. The consumption of nature thus becomes a *cause*.

Now, whether many of our pioneer forefathers on this continent did or did not act in daily dread of this particular interpretation of the scriptures I do not know. I doubt it; I think the subdual style – conquer in the name of the Lord – is more appropriate to the Calvinist persuasion. I know that from their day to ours there has been an aura of godliness about the sensitive treatment of certain natural phenomena, most particularly soils; however, sanctimoniousness in wildlife conservation affairs has not usually been notable. The "sacred trust" notion has not moved much beyond agriculture. There has, however, been an interesting recent increase in participation on the part of theologians writing on broader matters of environmental concern that tends to echo the "stewardship" theme.

There is another important element. If service to the greater system (the biological continuity) is blessed, so too must be service to our descendants. Stewardship is most easily understood and accepted, I think, when suggested in the context of our children, and theirs. Entreaties on behalf of my offspring are more likely to commend my interest than those more nebulously stated. I am even moved, perhaps, to respond to entreaties on behalf of *your* children. The obligation to future generations is one few would disavow. It is a compelling appeal – to the point of occasional triteness.

Although we hear of this obligation too often from the lips of politicians and we read it too frequently on the letterheads of private organizations, it is rare for anyone to fly in the face of it. If motherhood is no longer quite so sacred as it once was, our duty to those human beings now in place and to be anticipated in future is inescapable. If you won't do it for yourself, or even for the greater biological or theological purpose, you will do it for future generations. You have the right to use nature in your own time, and you have the duty to pass it on in at least as good shape as it was when you received it – preferably better. Thus, the good steward of natural resources, including wildlife, is enjoined by God, by contemporary conservationists, and by those not yet born. This is not a threat of reprisal. It is a matter of conscience.

Sustainable Harvest

Here, still in the rural mode, the self-interest of the good husbandman is again the major theme. The appeal is more direct and perhaps more effective because it involves a shorter time frame than the stewardship notion, offering a more immediately foreseeable dividend than mere husbandry for its own and your future sake. The concept of harvest is one everyone can grasp, or could grasp in the days before urban concentration, when the figure of speech was first used with respect to wildlife.

Although its origin is obviously agricultural, the harvest metaphor was addressed most particularly to those who kill either for recreation or for profit. It is chiefly they and their advocates, agents, and creatures in government service who continue to use it today. The rationale is quite simple. Most plants and animals produce in a given year more offspring than their environment can support. The codfish and the lobster are well-known examples. In nature, this seems to be a form of life insurance. If some unusual or catastrophic set-back were to strike the breeding population, there is an available pool from which fast recruitment may come. In most years this reserve is not required, and it is resorbed by the system. It is recycled. In the case of game species, this is termed the "harvestable surplus." Wise use of the resource indicates that this "surplus" may be taken without affecting capital. Each breeding season, then, produces such a dividend to be "harvested" for fun and profit. Otherwise, it would be "wasted."

"Harvest" is–or was, in earlier times–a compelling thought in North America. There was much traditional joyful imagery attached to it: bounty, togetherness, colour, turkeys, cider, pumpkins, wheat sheaves, hay rides, and all the rest of it. Bringing in the cornucopia. We were raised on it, and most of us have warm, positive cultural images of harvesting. Even if it is little more than folklore it is appealing. (As in most orgies of nostalgia, we forget about the work that was involved in the good old days.)

It is interesting that in Britain, which did not experience the North American variant of Protestantism, and where space dictates that agriculture is quite different, the euphemism for sport killing is "culling." Culling is a gardener's word, not a farmer's. It is the selection of individual plants in a bed, not the wholesale reaping of them. Presumably the British figure of speech is just as useful to the "sporting" community as our own.

The fact that the "harvest" metaphor is still everyday talk in North America, especially among those concerned with species that are killed for human recreation, is testimony to its effectiveness when you remember that in the biosphere there is no harvestable surplus of anything. Waste is unknown. All of that reservoir of organic material that is not brought into breeding populations is fed back into the system. That "excess" *is* the support system. It is food, chemical compounds, nutrients. It fuels the very processes that sustain breeding populations and give rise to next year's.

Significantly, the wolf that takes the caribou or the falcon that takes the teal or the whale that grazes the krill is never seen to be "harvesting." Presumably that is because that individual consumer simply takes what comes its way and has no conscious investment in it. The meaning of "harvest" is that someone worked, usually very hard, for it. Someone planted and cultivated and tended and hoed and watered and raised it. These the wolf and the falcon and the whale clearly did not do. That the "sport" shooter did no more is also clear.

Profound implications regarding the relationship of man and wildlife notwithstanding, the "harvest" argument works, and has worked for several generations. That it continues to work so effectively today has certain other significance, to which I shall return.

Essentially, the notion of "harvesting" is a logical extension of the "husbandry" argument in a way that has much more immediacy and apparently wider appeal than mere caretaking.

Future Resources

Here we have a further development of both husbandry and harvest themes. Although cast in the future, it must derive its substance from the past. Earlier generations of harvesters unwisely consumed all of the passenger pigeons, great auks, Labrador ducks, and Carolina parakeets, and most of the Eskimo curlews, bison, pronghorns, sea otters, grey whales, and many more. Their treatment of those "resources" was unintelligent by today's standards and we have been the poorer for it. The fact that this generation is in the process of using up most of the Atlantic salmon, African elephants, and all of the blue whales, will no doubt be described as unwise and unintelligent by the next.

This argument, however, was not originally and is not now restricted to wildlife. It applies across the "resource" spectrum and, indeed, may find application with some of the so-called "non-renewables," to which most of the notions of conservation as a dynamic activity seem inappropriate. A snake-up of the plastics industry, for example, might at least prolong if not guarantee the supply of crude oil and other organic substances for more appropriate purposes.

As it applies to wildlife, this injunction is not much different from its fellows in the "wise use" category. It underlines utility; it perceives resources as exclusively human property; it tries to emphasize good husbandry and common sense. It is sane, sound, and something short of inspirational. It assumes self-interest, and that we have both the capacity and the will to extend our self-interest beyond our individual lives. It is not what the young would call a "grabber."

Science

This aspect of the "self-interested wise use" argument is much more recent than all of the foregoing. It arose later, and is thus more "relevant"; its appeal is strong in most quarters today. I remember when I first encountered it, many years ago, I thought that at last here was ammunition that seemed very promising indeed. Used judiciously, it would help to transcend the rural folksy mode in which (quite properly, in its time) conservation had been cast; it would appeal to those who simply were not interested in compost heaps and watersheds and tree farming and topsoils and trout hatcheries, but who *were* interested in the advancement of human power in the universe through science. In other words, here appeared to be the beginning of an argument that just might allow wildlife preservation to penetrate the meticulously ordered anthropocentric world of high civilization. Wildlife as the precious raw material of sacred science! It gave me a marvellous morale-boosting lift at the time.

The argument is logically straightforward. If you lose something before you have a chance to study and understand it—even an animal or plant species—then not only you but all of science (human knowledge) will be the poorer. This is where the judicious use comes in. You do not publicly advocate preserving the hairy-nosed wombat for the sake of science, because nobody will take you seriously. But you do advocate the preservation of tropical forests, which contain plants of potentially inestimable worth as, perhaps, poisons or cosmetics. If you let these forests go, who knows what might be lost to mankind, forever? If you lose the sea lion or the fur seal before you understand the biochemical processes of delayed implantation (of the fertilized egg in the uterus), who can tell what alleviation or indeed enhancement of the human condition will have been denied to us? And so on.

This appeal – and it is a reasonably persuasive one even in circles where the notion of wildlife preservation is without meaning otherwise – is of course packaged in utilitarian terms. Although the argument is made in terms of pure science, and is thus of the highest respectability, the real message is to application-technique. This is where much of its strength lies. Even the most impatient and headstrong among the technocrats acknowledges that technique arises out of "pure" science, and that in the final analysis man's mastery of the observable world depends on man's ultimate knowledge of that world. Thus is the appeal for conservation made respectable in contemporary terminology. The benefit to wildlife is slim.

Very recently, this argument has been extended in ways that were undreamed-of in my earlier experience. Ecology, the study of the process inter-relationships of living beings in their environments, has become one of the most popular of sciences. It exists also as an "applied" science. The "wise use for the good of science" argument has allowed many varieties of ecologic research to develop, on the grounds that if you do not know how the biophysical system works, then your chances of manipulating that system in the advancement of human affairs are limited. This has much strengthened the impetus to preserve natural areas, often as representative examples of various habitat types. The appeal is made in entirely utilitarian terms, but there are incidental benefits to both plant-animal associations and to individual species.

Pure knowledge has been the sometimes unintended beneficiary of the relatively new activity that has come to be known as "environmental impact assessment." EIA, as it is known among its practitioners, is interesting and enlightening. When some grandly glittering construction scheme is proposed, appropriate governmental authority may require that a token investigation be made of its possible social, economic, biologic, or ecologic consequences. (The political results will have been weighed well before the plan is made public.) In the process of such investigation, information may be uncovered that may be of no interest whatever to the proponents of the project, nor indeed to the bureaucrats, but that may add to the pool of information. Thus we have gained knowledge, it must be said, that we would never have gained without the funding that surrounds large building projects. Wise use – here meaning ecologic field studies – can indeed mean the advancement of science.

The quality of science so delivered, however, may be variable. Bad science as well as good science emerges. Many people have observed that the slapdash way in which so much of this slickly packaged work is done and the casual level of review to which it is subjected are open invitations to disaster, both for science and for wildlife.

Wildlife preservation can never be an effective argument for the undertaking of these sorts of studies. Since the reasons for the studies themselves are entirely political (strategic, or in many cases, merely tactical), the guardianship of wildlife populations, species, or associations is never a factor in a motivational sense. But, like the good Presbyterians we conservationists are, we long ago learned to accept the collection plate as it comes, and not to ask too many questions.

EIA is a grandiloquent fraud, a hoax, and a con. Others have seen it as both a boondoggle and a subterfuge. It is one of the deceitful co-options of the concepts of ecology and environment of which I spoke earlier. While sanctimoniously reciting the catechism of "environmentalism," it anoints and blesses the process of "development," takes the initiative from the preservationists, and, in most cases, effectively bulldozes, gravels, and hardtops the road for the technomachine. Ecology is thus used as a tool to permit "developers" to continue to do what they have always done. The only difference is that "environmental impact is to be minimized to an acceptable level." What is minimal impact? What is acceptable impact? Acceptable to whom? Wildlife, alas, cannot be interviewed.

EIA may not be good science, and it may not be conservation, but it is excellent business. Like its cousins, the regional master plan and the evaluation of land capability, it does contrive to circulate much money, the tab for which you and I, and the silent majority that is wildlife, will ultimately pay. Also, it tends to shore up the ancient human hallucination having to do with the predictability and thus the controllability of all things.

The scientific argument for wildlife conservation has come to be widely used in a somewhat unexpected quarter–zoos. Many modern zoos have made much of the need to protect (and of course to display) critically rare or endangered species, as a contribution to the larger conservation movement. Historically, as the supply of new and replacement (the turnover in some of the newest establishments is appalling) animals from the wild began to dry up dramatically, zoos were forced to develop captive breeding programs of their own, for a relatively few species. This had immediate results in veterinary medicine, among other applied sciences. It also had "box-office" value arising from the publicity surrounding a list of endangered species such as the great apes, some antelopes, and others. Such publicity is generated (albeit in quite different forms) both by conservation organizations and by the zoos themselves. The benefit to the zoo is obvious; the benefit to wildlife conservation, so long as the animals remain captive and are not released to the wild, is zero. Indeed, natural habitat destruction may proceed at an accelerated rate now that the public has been assured that the species is "safe." The benefit to some aspects of scientific and technical knowledge is said to be considerable.

Here we have again the utilitarian theme (research, education), although in this case pure knowledge is most frequently identified as the contribution of zoos. Also, of course, we have wildlife as "resource" in the usual sense of human proprietorship—in this case for captive display in the interest of entertainment. Again, the fact that we have neglected to interview the animals by way of opinion survey is somehow overlooked.

"Wise Use" in Summary

"Wise use" is the hard, germinal kernel of the self-interest approach to wildlife conservation argument. Wildlife is a renewable resource. Treated wisely and intelligently, it can benefit today's users and those of future generations. Your right of access to the resource is accompanied by a duty, not to the resource, but to today's and tomorrow's publics. The resource is yours to enjoy and to protect. The careful use of the resource is not only prudent but also, in a human ethical sense, obligatory.

Throughout, wildlife is seen solely as a human asset. There is not the slightest question of any intrinsic interest being vested in wildlife itself. It is a human commodity.

THE "QUALITY OF LIFE" ARGUMENT

This approach has emerged more recently as a popular argument for wildlife preservation, although the poets have expressed it metaphorically for centuries. Still very near to the core of the self-interest sphere, it tends to take as given most of the "wise use" implications (husbandry, responsibility, future generations), but it concentrates on a qualitative as opposed to a measurable payoff. In general, this argument has enjoyed its greatest effectiveness and success in realms that are very remote from the wildlife question—toxic pollution, urban horrors, the population blight, industrial indecencies, and recreational demands.

This one meshes well (indeed much better than "wise use" can do) with the conventional picture of a civilized society. Life quality as a notion rests well with many branches of our society that are relatively untouched by rural and wildland imagery. Because the overwhelming majority of us are city-dwellers and, as such, are especially sensitive to the comforts and discomforts of an entirely fabricated environment, the "quality of life" argument may be easily carried in terms that everyone understands – physical amenities, arts and letters, social relationships – the humanistic tradition generally.

What does this have to do with preservation of wildlife? At first glance, very little. But there are ways. For one thing, the protection of nature is something that obviously befits the sensitive and genteel human being. Because many perceptions of life quality have strong narcissistic overtones, it suits the individual and collective self-image to patronize "those who cannot speak for themselves" in much the same way as we would patronize the arts and sciences. Or the poor, needy, and afflicted. It is the proper thing to do. This can be used – not as an argument, of course, because it is not one – but it can be used as a device.

Among conservationists the quality of life concept is very often expressed in terms of *environmental* quality. This helps to narrow the focus slightly, especially if we are then able to suspend the wider sociocultural aspects of "environment" to concentrate on the biophysical. But even here there is a problem. Virtually everyone seems to agree on "environmental quality" as a valid policy goal, but I have not yet seen a firm definition of what it means. This is an important hindrance.

You and I may agree on many things, but we will not agree on all things. Our appreciations of environmental quality may be absurdly different. The arctic is of very high environmental quality for seals, but of very low quality for flamingoes. The contemporary urban environment is of very high quality for rats and roaches, but of very low quality for moose and for millions of people.

You might be tempted to take issue with this, on the grounds that the notion of "quality" is entirely inappropriate and indeed irrelevant to an animal's ability to survive in a given natural situation. Of course a flamingo cannot survive in the arctic, you say. Either an animal is adapted to a given environment or it is not; the question has nothing to do with "quality." In response to this, I would thereupon leaf through my field guide and identify you as a species of 'ologist, seeing all things through reductionist human eyes, and denying the capacity for qualitative experience in all beings except human beings. I would accuse you of taking craven refuge in "objectivity," which in my book is listed under cop-outs. I choose to believe that nonhuman beings *do* perceive quality and its absence in their environments, and that they behave accordingly. Watch a wolf in a cage; watch a porpoise in the open sea.

Even if we were to adopt a completely self-interested (anthropocentric, as opposed to biocentric) definition of environmental quality, your quality would almost certainly not be mine, nor mine yours. I think that both of us, however, would feel that environmental quality involves at least some element of choice, something having to do with keeping the options open. (This implies that we are able to recognize options for what they are – possibly a foolhardy assumption.)

To the naturalist, environmental quality means, among other things, heterogeneity. It means variety, diversity, options. Homogeneity (uninterrupted wheat fields, tree farms, cities, highways, feedlots) is a kind of ecologic heresy. The concept of a healthy ecosystem is one with many parts, many roles, many inter-relationships, many alternatives, many structures and functions, many ways of doing things. It is dynamic and it flows and changes. The resilient ecosystem provides options for its parts and processes in the event of disturbance. It has escape valves. The monoculture, on the other hand – the pure culture of Scots pine, rice, or people – is an open invitation to disease, parasitism, and destruction. The reduction of parts and processes, roles and alternatives, can weaken a system and make it vulnerable. The same is true, obviously, of a society or a culture.

Life quality means life options, options for change. To the student of evolutionary biology, every variation in every individual organism is an option for change. It may not be "used" immediately – or ever – but it is there, against possibilities. Evolution is opportunistic: new variations, each of which is an individual "experiment," continually probe and test the changing environment for new opportunities. When the option presents itself, a new variant may become a new ecotype, a new race, perhaps even a new species. There are variations in anatomy, in physiology, and in behaviour. These variations evolve, in concert with changing environments, over time.

There are variations also in human cultures, beliefs, values, traditions, assumptions, even perceptions. Or rather there used to be. The culture of the western technomechanistic (we sometimes call it "developed!") world seems to me to be pathetically homogeneous. A colossal irony is that we apparently perceive this homogeneity (one world–in our image) to be good. On the other hand, the "quality of life" argument implies that there may be options.

I readily grant that the connection with wildlife preservation is getting tenuous here, except for those who see wildlife as a desirable option, the existence of which can contribute to their particular model of life quality. This has never been a strong contender in an operational sense. Wildlife can be an unintended beneficiary, however, as, for example, when pieces of attractive landscape are set aside for scenic or recreational purposes. Here, those forms of animal and plant life that are able to tolerate whatever intensity of human use develops, persist. And of course there are those animals desired for the killing which are carefully "husbanded" as part of the life quality of their peculiar human constituency.

Here I would tentatively venture to explore a more expanded notion of "life quality" which is not yet a stock argument. This is the biocentric approach. It is advocated by numerous individuals but not, I fear, sufficiently widely or intelligibly to be of much significance yet. (This is not to suggest that I disagree with it–on the contrary–merely to say that at the moment it has gone exactly nowhere.) In this approach, "quality" is simply the phenomenon of living, of which man is a part, but only a part. The quality lies in the richness of the life experience *within* flows and forms and processes that are not of human manufacture and that function as a total and heuristic happening. The experience lies in being in and part of it. As the richness and variety of the environmental whole are reduced, simplified, and degraded by human activity, so the richness and variety of the individual human life experience are proportionately affected. In this case "quality" becomes the maintenance of the life complex in all of its manifestations, allowing the process to exercise its own options, as it always did in prehuman times. All this in the interest of fuller human experience.

This starts to drift toward the ethical argument, which will be discussed later. Since we are still, at this stage, in the realm of human self-interest, perhaps I should not bring up ethics at all. However, ethics, whether classical or not, seem to carry with them at least the promise if not the presence of reciprocity. It might be that the fullest human experience can only be realized in an ethical approach to the living surround; that it would be in our own interest. More of this in a more appropriate place.

This is the right place, however, for a look at the *aesthetic* argument for life quality as it contributes to the human self-interest.

The benefit to the individual beholder is vivid and present. There are many compelling arguments for wildlife framed only in terms of beauty. Much of this is delivered to us by way of graphic art, including photography. (This is not to deny the long tradition of "nature writing," of which I shall have something to say later; I am thinking of our special primate fondness for visual immediacy.)

Much if not most of the conventional aesthetic argument for wildlife is presented not only in visual terms but also in environmental context. It is easier to present the aesthetic appeal of a walrus in the dazzling shimmer of silver and blue and green that surrounds it, than in silhouette. It is the frozen lake and its looming rim of spruce that make the wolf "real." Even the bird-of-paradise looks better against its deep and lightless jungle backdrop than in vignette. What is really "sold" in pictorial wildlife aesthetics is the natural environment, not its pieces. For its part, the bird-of-paradise "completes" the forest scene, makes it whole. I suspect most people, when admiring the appearance of a leopard in a zoo, project it back into its native forest. Many people feel sad at a zoo. That too is an aesthetic experience.

The beauty of aesthetics is that in spite of our infatuation with opinion surveys it cannot be quantified. Aesthetics does not rely for its respectability on supporting hard data. (In view of this, one occasionally wonders how it is that in the present time aesthetics contrives to survive at all!) Apart from its original meaning as a branch of philosophy having to do with "the beautiful," aesthetics is largely a matter of individual human perception. To this extent the value of aesthetics is heightened – or lessened – according to one's individual perceptual predisposition.

In classical aesthetics, the beauty of a thing is weighed by comparison with its "ideal archetype" – its prototype or model – itself often a stereotype, or what we might call an institutionalized image. It is the product of cultural convention. It changes over time, but slowly. Hence the difficulty, it would appear, experienced by the creator of atonal music or cubist portraiture or pointillist landscape or geodesic domes in cracking the vested resistance to change. Each of us varies from the cultural norm in these things, but not much. Even though aesthetics is very much in the eye, ear, and mind of the individual experiencer, that experiencer has been well and truly conditioned by the traditional cultural environment. The possibility of aesthetics being much more than pure "nurture" seems to me very remote. (No doubt the aesthetic *capacity* is inherent in us; the content is inserted.) Every creative artist knows how calcified, rigid, and unyielding culturally institutionalized images of "the beautiful" have a way of becoming.

At the present time, the (visual) aesthetic appeal for wildlife is packaged almost entirely in conventional landscape. We are receptive to it because it is in the cultural background. Traditional landscape aesthetics, of course, has nothing whatever to do with wildlife, but it is often influenced by the presence or absence of man. A somewhat dismaying (because it is probably accurate) formula has been put forward by Nan Fairbrother: landscape = habitat + man. It is, as she says, an unstable equation because it is forever changing–changed by a creature who is himself changing. Landscape, she points out, is not a static background, but the interaction of a society and the habitat it lives in. All is change.

As a naturalist I am very much aware of the process of change, and so I feel that in that sense Fairbrother is absolutely correct. Nothing can be static; even institutionalized images can change over time. What *is* however alarmingly close to static is the perceived central role of man in all things, even landscape. That particular hallucination is firm.

From the traditional point of view we hear a great deal more about "man in the landscape" than we do about simple "landscape." To the committed humanist observer, a landscape may be "empty" if man or the evidence of man is missing. At the very least he will want to see the *potential* for man in that landscape. Thus the arctic tundra is a wasteland, the moon barren and empty. A landscape may only be "complete" if man or the evidence of man or the potential for man is somewhere visible or capable of being inferred. To the wilderness "purist," on the other hand, man (except in very low numbers and of course except for himself) may not be appropriate at all.

Usually we seem to discover the "man in the landscape" aesthetic at its most mature development, where man has been in residence for hundreds or thousands of years, to a point at which human evidence, in the appreciative observer's eye, is part of the landform itself. A point where man is "in harmony" with landscape. Spain comes to mind here. But we are never told what "harmony" means. If it means the man-induced Mediterranean deserts or the horizon-to-horizon rice paddies of the far east, then the euphony escapes me, because there nature has been wholly subdued and nowhere shows her face. Wildlife has long since been almost entirely eradicated. As far as human settlements are concerned, "man in harmony with nature" is meaningless gibberish, despite the facility and frequency with which we intone it.

All the same, we like to keep *technical* man's works in perspective. On a Precambrian lake, a canoe "belongs"; a motorboat does not. On the same lake in winter, a dogsled is appropriate; a snowmobile is not. In a forest landscape, the loggers should be using horses, not tractors. I am not going to pursue this further, except to suggest that there is a very long and deep romantic tradition involved here – very Anglo, I think – and it is just as misleading as most other frontier folklore.

Generally, wildlife species become the incidental – almost accidental – beneficiaries of the appreciation of the aesthetic properties of their immediate habitats. They benefit not because there is an ideal archetype of the living being itself. Admittedly some animals (male deer, Canada geese, mallards) and white pines qualify. But they are overwhelmed by cattle, wheat, grain elevators, sailboats, cottages, decoys, kayaks, and people. Here, to the hairy-nosed wombat problem I would add the stinkpot turtle problem. Most wildlife species are not represented by ideal archetypes in our cultural catalogue.

In spite of this, for generations there have been artists who specialized in animals, and whose work has ranged from the most highly technical scientific illustration to the full-fledged elegance of creative portraiture, even impressionism. Several superb practitioners are active today. I feel, however, that in the world of art appreciation their recognition has come more from their talents than from their subject matter. They paint wildlife because they love wildlife, but they also happen to be artists of the first rank. In the salons, the content may well be incidental. I have found no sparking synapse between animal art and operational wildlife preservation.

Within limits, however, the aesthetic argument for wildlife is good. It is attractive to the self-interest in the sense that it adds new or reveals latent options for "life quality." It is most effective, one would suppose, with those who have had prior experience of the phenomenon pictured, either directly or indirectly.

It always seems a bit strange that, when reviewing our sundry aesthetic models, there does not seem to have developed any culturally accepted archetype of the beautiful in terms of such non-visual abstracts as *process*. The nearest thing we seem to have is the appreciation of form in music or poetry or dance –

form, as opposed to specific content. This, as a kind of process, we understand and appreciate aesthetically. But we have not developed an aesthetic of *life* process. That is because our culture is essentially abiotic.

The life system – the process – is beautiful. Anything that tends to simplify or obstruct or alter or damage the process is unbeautiful. A wounded, limping life process, like a rotting city core, is ugly. That which is ugly may quite properly be described as disadvantageous to the system. (We may be either self-interestedly anthropocentric here, or biocentric, when we speak of the "support" system.) This is not merely a value statement; it is a factual statement. We are surrounded by the evidence of it. We live in the evidence of it.

Some years ago I chose as my archetype of the *un*beautiful the 45-gallon fuel drum. On the arctic tundra it not only looks like a suppurating chancre on the cheek of Mona Lisa, but also its implications for wildlife everywhere in the world are hideous. If you want a symbol, there it is. I find it more informative than a cute cartoon of a giant panda. There are many other such examples, according to your individual experience, perspective, and predilection.

In sum, the "quality of life" argument for the preservation of wildlife stresses human options, chiefly experiential, and offers a variety of plants, animals, and environments as rich potential fare in the individual and collective interest. A future orientation is implicit if not always stated. It is very weak on life process. The use is "nonconsumptive," but the notion of proprietorship remains firm. The flow of benefits continues to be one way.

THE "ECOCATASTROPHE" (DOOMSDAY) ARGUMENT

This is the scare strategy – the most brutally direct of the self-interest approaches to conservation. It glosses over nothing, etching possible futures in stark and bold relief. There is no waffling, no circling, no obliqueness, little euphemism. This, ladies and gentlemen, is the way it is – or the way it is going to be – unless... Heavy handed, perhaps, but refreshingly straightforward and free of rationalization. An apparent weakness is that it assumes that people will listen – and act.

The "gloom and doom" formula, which all of us have toyed with at one time or another, is too familiar to require more than brief mention. In a very real way it reminds me of the evangelical technique of earlier times: scare the living bejesus out of them; then, with exquisite timing, flourish the recipe for salvation. For maximum effectiveness it depends on equal measures of belief and doubt on the part of the audience; hard evidence is secondary.

With or without a litany of facts, the salvationist works on uncertainty, and sells immortality insurance on that basis. But of course what the fire-and-brimstone preacher is digging at is *individual* fear, *personal* fear. I know of no way in which the tribulations of wildlife can scare anyone. The fact that evidence of *human* peril surrounds us (indeed the evidence fairly overwhelms those who understand what they see in front of them) should make the delivery of his payload somewhat easier for the ecocatastrophist than for the salvationist. But it does not. Billy Graham draws bigger crowds than Paul Ehrlich. Belief is a question we shall get into later.

The doomsday argument should be potent. There are problems the magnitude of which we can barely envisage at this stage, and worse is yet to come, unless...This is surely the ultimate appeal to the self-interest. So far as I can determine, it has absolutely no relevance to wildlife preservation. When human survival is at last on the line, the priorities will become strikingly clear. Wildlife could of course emerge as a second-generation beneficiary should we choose to listen to the ecocatastrophists and take evasive action in the interest of our own skins. This is not, however, part of the argument, either for wildlife or for the self-interest.

ABOUT SELF-INTEREST

Before we go further, it will be useful to sum up those arguments for conservation that are based in individual and collective human self-interest, as put forward here. The most fundamental message is: *if we can't be good, at least we can be prudent.* The message has been delivered historically and is delivered today in a number of ways: the "wise use" arguments involve husbandry, stewardship, harvest, future resources, science, and technology; the "quality of life" argument stresses present and future options and aesthetics; the "ecocatastrophe" or "doomsday" argument is essentially "act now or pay later."

The guts of the self-interest family of arguments is that they are entirely and exclusively man-oriented, anthropocentric. Whether it is directed to individual, group, nation, or species, the appeal is to the human being and the human interest. The future may also be presented in the form of subsequent human generations. We may frame the argument either in the investment-dividend or the waste-bankruptcy mode; the metaphor may vary, but the message is the same.

Throughout, we assume nature as "resource," whether for physical use or as a source of aesthetic enjoyment. In this sense, living sensate wildlife beings are no different from water, soils, and landforms, all of which were set in place by a beneficent nature expressly for human purposes. Whether man is good steward or renegade, whether answerable to God or to the biosystem or to future human generations or not, there is no question about the locus of vested power and authority on Earth. This is illustrated best, I think, in the monumentally dull-witted arrogance of the concept of "harvest" as applied to wildlife species.

In almost all cases, save commercially or technically important species, which are commodities, the role of wildlife is that of incidental or spin-off beneficiary from "resource management" policies and practices. Even in aesthetics (endangered species excepted), wildlife benefits as landscapes and wildlands benefit, rarely for its own sake.

For its logical integrity, the self-interest argument *must* see wildlife as a "resource," a commodity, a utility. This brings us back to the distinction between "renewable" and "non-renewable" resources. I no longer believe that there is, in practice, such a thing as a "renewable" resource. Once a thing is perceived as having some utility – any utility – and is thus perceived as a "resource," its depletion is only a matter of time. I know of no wildlife that is being "renewed" anywhere – not yellow birch or hemlock or anchovies or marlins or leopards or salmon or bowhead whales or anything else. "Renewable resource" is self-contradictory incoherence, at least as applied to wildlife.

If "resource" continues to mean something that is put to human use, then no resource is renewable. Our demands have quite outstripped the capacity of those resources to satisfy them, much less to satisfy them on a "sustainable" basis. And we are, of course, never satisfied. Our insatiability is a vast subject and one I cannot get into here, except to remind you that there is no scrap of evidence, anywhere, to indicate that demands can be reduced. All of our efforts are directed toward increasing *supply*. Almost all, that is; the "sporting" and recreational industries do put considerable effort into beefing up demand. The best we seem to be able to do in the way of "renewing" something is to stop consuming it for a while and hope that nature will do the rest.

In our society, if a thing has value then it *must be used*. Otherwise we could not put a value to it. The word "value" as applied to wildlife derives from the *utilitarian imperative*, which is a part of our imperialistic stance toward nature as a whole. This underlies even the scientific-technical argument for wildlife preservation: who knows what uses might be discovered one day? Ironically enough, it is also implicit in the familiar "*No use* is a legitimate *use*." Now this one is very glib and very fine on the surface, but it freely admits that conservation must present *all* of its case in the utilitarian mode. This is more than saddening; it is frightening. Conservation, far from confronting the utilitarian imperative, chooses to legitimize it and argue from it. This, for our movement, I perceive as a species of death wish.

With very precise (commercial) exceptions, the self-interest argument has not and cannot preserve wildlife. It can perpetuate some specifically desired or most-favoured forms, no more. The preservation of wildlife *for its own sake*, with no implication of use, is antithetical to the self-interest position. By its very emphasis on the utilitarian imperative, the latter drives the conceptual wedge between man and nature ever deeper, thus reducing the possibility of the achievement of wildlife preservation in the ideal sense. This is not a comforting thought, for many conservationists would claim that self-interest is the only argument we have.

The only wildlife that can be (conventionally) *proven* to be in the human self-interest are commercial species that we can describe in dollar terms. Dollar values are attached to individuals of certain endangered species in the zoo trade also. Beyond this we have the very nebulous category of those wildlife forms desired for aesthetic (quality) reasons, which in most instances centre on landscapes and recreational possibilities rather than individual species.

The overwhelming mass of wildlife species are not at present commercially desirable, and although the list of rare and threatened species is depressingly long, it is not yet great relative to the absolute number of plant and animal species that are still with us. But it grows rapidly. It is my waking nightmare to think that a species must be either commercially valuable or endangered in order to be seriously considered for active protection. But if one persists in seeing wildlife as a "resource," and thus in accepting the burden of demonstrating its utility in the human interest, this is where the argument must necessarily and inevitably lead. There is no escape.

To this point, apart from a brief note, we have not looked at those uses of wildlife usually termed "non-consumptive." For many years wildlife conservationists, for purposes of argument and explication, drew a distinction between those activities that actually "consumed" wildlife and those that did not. The distinction was useful at one time because it tended to underscore the need for different approaches to wildlife "management" under different circumstances and conditions, and especially to emphasize the need for protection of non-commercial species in the interest of a body of people who wanted wildlife for "passive" recreational purposes, no more. Simply for the viewing.

This was fine just as long as there were not too many people who wanted wildlife simply for the viewing. It will not be necessary here to go into all the recent revelations about the physical impact of the tourist stampede on parks, sanctuaries, and game reserves all over the world. Recreational ("non-consumptive") uses have become an enormous problem. Indeed there is no such animal as the "non-consumptive" user of wildlife. We are having to "retire" campsites even in Canada, where there is alleged to be infinite room. To my certain knowledge, a succession of zebra-striped vans with their loads of instamatic-bearing tourists is infinitely more damaging to the ground cover and thus to the *total* biosystem in African parks than any wretched psychotic in his Abercrombie and Fitch hunting costume can possibly be. This we know. The volume and the impact of tourism in all parts of the world are absolutely staggering.

Just as I can no longer see wildlife as a "renewable resource," I can no longer think of a "non-consumptive" use of wildlife. If it is a use, it consumes. The terms are archaic and no longer have meaning; worse, the arguments they imply are destructive of the goal itself. By suggesting that wildlife is "renewable" you sanctify the notion of "management," you confirm and ratify the assumed role of wildlife in the service of man, and you also imply that it *is* in fact being renewed. Nothing could be more misleading, or fallacious. By suggesting that recreational uses of wildlife other than outright killing are "non-consumptive" you overlook and thus worsen recreational impact, and once again you legitimize the utilitarian imperative.

It seems that such notions as renewability and non-consumptiveness actually contradict the real goals of wildlife preservation. The standard self-interest argument, even at the aesthetic level, acknowledges no earthly role or place for wildlife beyond the human interest, no existence beyond the human purpose. If not overtly, certainly by implication, it nurtures a perception of wildlife that is radically at odds with preservation. The very attitudes the argument perpetuates have always been our chief obstacle. This is the "loop" into which we have fallen.

Most important, in a practical sense, the utilitarian argument leaves in limbo the huge majority of wildlife species for which no such value can be demonstrated. Dependence on the self-interest argument has knotted conservation in an impossible double bind, our stated case actually cementing us into our most basic problems. Such perhaps was not always the case, but it is today. To admit wildlife into the human cosmos solely as a commodity in the human interest is to make preservation an absolute impossibility.

Finally, self-interest is a risky approach in any case. It is well-known that practices in the self-interest have a way of being abandoned and forgotten if the predicted difficulty does not loom over the horizon soon enough to keep them alive. If the "danger" cannot be shown to be actual and immediate (and who, after all, would feel threatened by the extinction of the Cambodian kouprey or the New Caledonian kagu?), self-interest tends to evaporate as any kind of motive. The trumpets are not sounding the call to judgement just yet. We still have time.

The argument of self-interest is fundamentally contradictory to the wildlife preservation purpose, and in actuality works against that purpose. Its long tradition is one of the prime reasons for our failure.

Ethics

Rightly or wrongly, I have arbitrarily separated this examination of the ethical argument for wildlife from the self-interest section, to concentrate on pure altruism. Current "sociobiology" maintains that there is a deep and abiding vested genetic interest in nonhuman altruistic behaviour, but I choose to set that to one side for present purposes. Whether it is legitimate to consider ethics outside the realm of self-interest is open to question, perhaps, but I shall proceed regardless.

There has been much call for an "environmental ethic," and many good minds have spent much time in trying to come to grips with it. Most of this work has centred around the human (especially urban) environment, in much the same way as "quality of life" explorations have done. An ethical approach specifically in terms of wildlife is rare. Although an undefined "ethos" would seem to be the prime motivation of many of us, to the present time it has defied institutionalization among our organizations. This is not especially difficult to understand when we acknowledge that up until now ethics have been concerned almost exclusively with human individual-to-individual and individual-to-society relationships.

Although we do use the term "ethics" broadly and I think somewhat sloppily in our arguments on behalf of wildlife, we come back to the "quality of life" problem in that no one has yet advanced an acceptable (meaning workable) definition of what a wildlife ethic might look like. Ethics, in the non-academic sense, are simply principles of good or moral behaviour. To urge a "wildlife ethic" is merely an injunction to behave morally or decently toward wildlife. This would have a variety of possible interpretations through the perceptual spectrum of the sundry vested human interests in wildlife. Also, it does not help us much in the absence of background on what sort of behaviour might be considered good, moral, or proper, from the point of view of wildlife. We cannot ask them. The Golden Rule of a Tasmanian devil might be at odds with that of a planarian, and there is some possibility that even the human mind might not be able to comprehend either.

Let us begin with some of the more conventional arguments, which may help in the search for implications and refinements.

OUR MORAL DUTY TO FUTURE GENERATIONS
When viewed in the ethical frame, this has slightly different meaning than it did in the self-interest context. We have discussed the notion of "stewardship" on behalf of our descendants—the obligation to hand over that which has been in our temporary custodianship in as good shape as we can manage. This is an entirely anthropocentric appeal, and an apparently useful one. If we try to move it somewhat beyond tangible self-interest (the bird actually in the hand), it becomes somewhat more appealing.

In a way, this becomes a kind of "quality of life" stewardship—a custodianship—not of material assets in the form of commodities, but of a set of choices or options. We have a moral duty not to foreclose options on behalf of those who will follow us. There is no shred of reciprocity involved in an ethical arrangement with those who are not going to be around until after our deaths, so in that sense at least this is an altruistic position. There is nothing in it for us; only for them. (That there may be for us a soupçon of private congratulation is forgiveable.)

The argument sounds even better when we acknowledge that we haven't the faintest idea, really, how future generations will *perceive* their options. Or indeed how they will perceive "resources." Perhaps they may well see values—or values of different kinds—in items which at the present time we either consider unimportant or fail to see at all. This possibility alone means a moral obligation not to subtract anything now that might be of either material or experiential value to our descendants. Remember–resources *become*.

One example. They tell us that there are so many of the strange boojum (cirio) trees left in Baja California because nobody has thought of any use for them. But the fact that they are "useless" now is no reason to assume that they are going to remain so in perpetuity. So save them; maybe somebody will want them some day, after we have exhausted everything else. There has got to be *some* use for them, or God would not have put them there. This is the utilitarian fundament of the self-interest argument. On the other hand, it might be possible to speculate that boojum trees represent a kind of experiential or qualitative value as yet unrecognized by most people. For certain the world is full of people who have never clapped eyes on one. It would be immoral of us, unethical, to deprive our descendants of that experiential option.

All of it finally hinges on what we consider to be fitting and appropriate options for human posterity. And of course the morality is toward them, not toward wildlife. So it is that we, in our ethical posture, magnanimously bequeath the entire world of nonhuman nature to our heirs and assigns, once again emphasizing the total proprietary interest of man–whether in a quantitative or a qualitative sense–over the "resource." The message is clear and unequivocal. The anthropocentric universe turns, still very much locked in place, no matter how circumspect our behaviour toward our human survivors.

ETHICS AND VALUES
These present an even more difficult tangle of problems–interesting ones. To behave ethically in our society means to behave in conformity with a set of principles having to do with morality and propriety, toward the greater social purpose. Almost everybody knows the rules, and almost everybody behaves accordingly. Breaches of the rules are considered gauche at the very least, criminal at the worst. In general, the system works, because all members of a society are assumed to have access to the ethical code.

However, when we begin to circle around the notion of a "wildlife ethic," we encounter brambles. Let us for the moment see the wildlife ethic as part of a larger, broader "environmental ethic," about which much has been written, more speculated. There is no denying the fact that any ethic, environmental or otherwise, must be expressed in human terms in order to be understood by most of us. Those human terms are of course the human social interest. This of necessity takes us right back to both the "stewardship" (wise use) and "quality of life" varieties of the self-interest argument. An ethical position having to do with the total environment is construed as an ethical position with relation to those human beings now and in future who must live in that environment. Wildlife, for reasons suggested earlier, is not an important factor here.

So we come to the tough question: what about an ethical position with regard to that part of the total environment that is not human and is not of human manufacture and is not seen to be in the human interest? Is it possible to conceive of an ethic that could be extended outward, as it were, from man to non-man? From human society to nonhuman society, or wild nature? This is a painfully difficult task, even to conceptualize, much less to express in words, still less to implement. Here I am assuming the degree of altruism that would be required to extend unilaterally such an ethic in the certain knowledge that no "normal" reciprocity can be expected.

Historically and traditionally, indeed perhaps ultimately, there is simply no meaning to "ethics" outside the human sphere. This should not come as a surprise to anyone. Even if I believe myself to feel supremely and wholly altruistic in my ethical behaviour toward others, the matter of reciprocity is fundamental. Even for the most saintly among us, there is at least a warm reflected glow. All—or at least a very large majority—of people in a society *must* behave ethically (according to the canons of that society) if the ethics of that society are to mean anything at all. Wild nature, however, does not know our rules and is unable to observe them.

I think that we cannot conceive of a society (a community of self-interest) that could extend beyond our species. Such a society would have an impossible prerequisite—an unequivocal acknowledgement of the *whole* inter-relationship between man and nature. Such an awareness, which would of necessity involve both intellect and intuition, does not exist to any discernible extent in humankind.

I fear, therefore, that when we speak of "environmental ethics" we are very much talking to ourselves. We mean much the same thing as we do in the "quality of life" argument— responsibility toward people. Now, if the self-interest of people indicates that certain policies and practices should be imple- mented in order to conserve and perpetuate the nonhuman ele- ments of our environment, then steps may well be taken, but not as an ethical stance toward those elements. It will be done in the self-interest. If the self-interest cannot be demonstrated, you may be certain that western society will develop no ethics with respect to nature.

It is obvious that the issue is essentially cosmological. The concept of the anthropocentric universe dictates everything that follows. As I have pointed out, the absence of an aesthetic for life process is part of the same problem. There is neither an ethical nor an aesthetic possibility for anything but a man-centred and man-ordered cosmos. That is what the technoculture is all about. The problem is metaphysical—not ethical, not aesthetic. The problem is the traditional western humanistic vision of man and his cosmological role.

As you begin to experience the full enormity of this problem, you will begin to fear that much of our effort in the proselytizing of the "wildlife ethic" is quite empty and fruitless. It is not that our audiences disagree with us or resent our argument or are offended by it: it means that *they cannot perceive it*. They literally do not know what we are talking about. To postulate rationally a cultural role for a nonhuman ethic would literally mean turning western metaphysics inside out, and that is a tall order, because it has to do with human purpose and meaning in the universe. I shall return to this.

One way of describing a set of ethical principles is to see it as mirroring the set of values shared by a society. In this sense, ethics and values are pretty much the same thing. We behave ethically toward those things we value; our modes of behaviour spring from those values in the first place; in turn, the ethical behaviour reinforces the values, and so on. This is a very tight lock-step relationship, the parts of which one really cannot separate. For these purposes I am going to pretend that I can, however, in order to look at the question of wildlife values.

There is much talk about the "value" of wildlife, from its aesthetic through recreational and economic to ecological value. These assessments are entirely arbitrary, of course, because they are attached to wildlife unilaterally by ourselves in the absence of dialogue with wildlife. All of us can find niches appropriate to our individual wildlife values. It is not so easy to find places or groupings for our social or cultural wildlife values. One generalization is possible: when we speak of wildlife values we mean values to us, not values to wildlife.

This seems reasonable enough, for it would be difficult to imagine that any species save man is capable of entertaining values as we understand them. A value, of course, does not exist in a vacuum; to be perceived at all it must be in a context. Usually it is a context in which we may apply such abstract (again, arbitrary) measures as good and bad, right and wrong. We like hierarchies: good, better, best. We are compulsive evaluators, in spite of the fact that our valuations have no reality whatever outside our own heads. I doubt that any species save man goes in for this obsessive accounting. I am fairly confident that nonhuman species do not need to entertain such odd concepts because they do not invest much time in rationalizing their appointed places in the perceived hierarchy of the cosmos. They do not seem to require that kind of reassurance.

Since values are abstractions, they have no concrete external reality, and like any other images can be changed at will. What *is* real, I suppose, is the *process* of valuing that goes on inside the individual human skull. I see myself forever entertaining notions that at least to me seem to have merit or usefulness, or that in my own egocentric universe may shed some positive light on me, the unique possessor of those particular notions. Or, I may well share a value – love of birds, let's say – with others, and in the standard pattern of group narcissism that value becomes a means of sorting out our hierarchic place relative to other groups, whom we are then able to perceive as philistines. Remember that "value" implies comparative measurement, whether we acknowledge it or not.

The values attached to wildlife by me or by anybody else have no existence outside our own minds, so we must admit that wildlife, like any other value, has no *intrinsic* worth. It has only the worth that you or I choose to give it. The value is an abstraction, a fabrication, an individual judgement only. Valuing wildlife from a broad social base could only result from large numbers of people sharing both the same perceptions and the same valuing process. Such synchrony is unlikely. The ultimate value, really, is in what the valuing process does for the individual valuer, no more than that. But that of course is everything.

It is interesting that in nature no price and no penalty seem to be attached to the individual existence. (We can and do conceptualize evolutionary and other biological and ecologic values, but these are pure fictions as well, not statements of real worth.) In nature there are no weird and bizarre notions like egalitarianism and the sacred individual to gum up the process. You merely spin out your time – eating, voiding, propagating, and eventually rejoining the system at a simpler level of organization. But since nothing goes away, there is no problem. An existence singularly free of hang-ups. The problem with valuing is that it attaches universal *meaning* to things.

In all honesty we must acknowledge that only a very modest fraction of people thinks about wildlife *at all*, even fleetingly, much less consciously attaches any value to it, still less ranks that value in any hierarchy of importance (vested interests in commercial species excepted). I am referring here to what we *do*, not what we say. When put to the test, any short-term human value you can name will operationally outweigh any long-term value, to say nothing of any nonhuman "value" of whatever time dimension.

Ethics and values, though interesting and indeed persuasive in an abstract theoretical sense, have little or no *practical* utility in the argument for wildlife preservation, as advanced presently. Perhaps one day, but time is not on the side of wildlife. Better, I think, to conserve our energies and creativeness toward something of more immediate promise. The ordered universe of humankind cannot admit turns of conceptual conduct as anomalous as these.

RIGHTS AND DUTIES

This consideration flows logically from ethics and values. Lately a number of people have begun to investigate possible avenues toward the identification of "rights" in an interspecific or even a systemic sense. If man has rights in respect to nature, surely the nonhuman has rights in respect to man. This speculation, perhaps too tenuous for serious contemplation by the confirmed liberal humanist, nevertheless has been usefully applied as a device with which to launch class-action legal process on behalf of a park, a forest, a water system, or something of that kind. Not yet a species, I suspect. However, I want to look at the question in the context of ethical behaviour by man toward wildlife. Does it contain the germ of an effective argument?

All concepts of rights are rooted in the value system of a society. The array of values to which a society adheres necessarily dictates a further array of duties and responsibilities that apply to both individuals and groups. The duties and responsibilities of the citizen are accompanied by appropriate rights. You have the right to be treated ethically and morally by your fellows, and at the grossest level you are also protected legally.

So we have the ethical structure of a society: you assume an obligation and receive an appropriate or concomitant right. If you work productively you eat well. Indeed you have the right to eat well nowadays, whether you work productively or not, which illustrates another contemporary value. Also children, the aged, and the insane have rights irrespective of any duties. The rights of "incompetents" spring from society's perceived obligation to them regardless of their productivity. That obligation springs in turn from a more fundamental value having to do with individual human lives.

We sometimes forget that every time a court or a legislature – or even custom – confers or confirms a right in someone, someone else's right is nibbled at: the right of women to equal employment opportunity is an infringement of the freedom of the misogynist employer; the right to make a profit is at someone else's cost; the right to run a motorcycle or a snowmobile reduces someone else's right to peace and quiet in his own backyard; the rights of embryos impinge upon the rights of the women who carry them. And so on.

As far as wildlife is concerned, our right to consume it now restricts subsequent generations' rights to consume it then. This is the essential argument of self-interest, and of "wise use." And, as it turns out, of ethics. Nothing can be comprehended outside the realm of human interest, because that is where the human perceptual apparatus stops. The thought of any inherent right in the nonhuman, which by definition would mean the restriction of a human right, is impossible in our culture.

The notion of right is untenable outside human society. One simple example will do. Leopard eats gazelle eats grass eats soil nutrients. If the gazelle had rights with respect to the leopard, the leopard would starve. If the grass had rights with respect to the gazelle, there would be no gazelle. Everything would shudder to a grinding halt forthwith. It does not work that way. The individual blade of grass, in its final ecstasy of self-actualization, knows that its roots are alive and well. Rich, nutrient-packed leopard droppings will be forthcoming shortly, and tomorrow there will be a new blade of grass.

A hierarchy of rights in nature would be a one-way street. The leopard *seemingly* has a right to the gazelle which *seemingly* has a right to the grass which in turn has a right to the soil which in turn has the right to and will eventually consume all of them. But do these rights actually exist? I think not, at least not so long as right implies concomitant duty. The only "duty" any living being owes is to the recycling machinery itself, and that duty is absolute. No one is exempt.

But that is a human perception only; it is not a conscious perception in nature. God sees the little sparrow fall in certain and secure knowledge that it is going straight into the hopper for feeding back into His greater system. He owes the sparrow nothing; the sparrow owes Him nothing. The only affront to God would be the sparrow's unilateral assumption of immortality, and God knows that is not in the greater scheme – not for sparrows nor for anyone else.

For us to argue that wildlife has inherent rights that should be respected by man would be just as faulty as the long-established and prevailing assumption that man has total right of access to wildlife. The sheer raw power of man makes it appear as though nature were acquiescing to some human right, but that is an appearance only. The only way in which nonhuman rights could be taken seriously would be to identify the appropriate duty in each transaction: a duty on the part of wildlife to man, a duty on the part of man to wildlife. Neither is sensibly thinkable.

The "rights of nature" cannot be a useful argument for wildlife preservation, because like so many of our other arguments, it turns upon itself. Nature knows no duty, therefore it can own no right. Still, as a stratagem against the time when the hierarchical concept of our relationship with the nonhuman is done with, it may have utility.

None of the traditional or even contemporary ethical arguments for wildlife preservation has yet been shown to be of the slightest practical value. In all ethics there must be the fundamental assumption that the underlying values, beliefs, duties, and obligations are fully, mutually understood, accepted, and shared. In speaking of ethics in the nonhuman context, we are jabbering into a void. Nature does not *need* ethics; there is no one to hear.

Spirituality

Here we have the polar opposite to the icy rationality of the argument of self-interest. Spirituality is less an argument, more a persuasion. It is individual and deeply personal and emotional. Conservationists have rarely used it in a broad way. They have preferred to attempt to present an ultra-logical case, with varying success. Usually the nearest we have allowed ourselves to drift in this direction has been through a kind of inspirational posture which, at times (especially at the individual level), may become "spiritual" in a very loose sense. There are frequent allusions to other powers and other dimensions, usually couched in generalities such as "the system," "the greater good," and so on. There seems to have been some reluctance to attempt to exploit the latent spirituality that is in every human being.

There are many reasons for this and perhaps they do not require elaboration here. Wildlife conservation groups and organizations tend to be highly heterogeneous in their composition. A substantial number (probably most) naturalists are not church-goers (no, I do not confuse church-going with spirituality), but virtually all of them have a deep emotional and spiritual feeling for wild nature in all its forms. I think conservation organizations have tended to shy away from any appearance of "using" this spirituality, even though between individuals and in small groups there is abundant sharing of the personal emotional experience. It would not be good policy on a public or mass basis, it is believed.

It certainly would not be good policy were the general public to continue to confuse sectarianism and other institutionalized believing for spirituality. In at least some quarters the wildlife preservationist is already seen as a kind of crank; to add to this any additional possibility of sectarian crankiness, as it is known in North American society, would be suicidal. Better, from a policy point of view, to leave the spiritual end of things, including "religious" experience, strictly alone. This is what we have done.

Even so, I cannot help wondering what the possibilities might be were we to uncover some germ of potential for wildlife preservation in the canons of one or another of the existing churches, of whatever stripe, for possible alliance. Not bloody likely. It is rather like politics. All conservationists have wailed and gnashed their teeth over the utter absence in the major political parties (or even the lesser ones) of any genuine commitment to conservation in the broadest (environmental) sense, much less in the more particular field of wildlife. Some of us have speculated whether we might actually form a political party dedicated to the advancement of the human good through environmental awareness and all of its appendages. (You would lose all your deposits in an election, but you would have had free time on television.) This, however, would only serve to alienate the rank and file of other political parties, and would be self-defeating. No doubt the same thing applies to organized religions; the conservationist has no wish to polarize spiritual positions.

There are few if any "all-purpose" appeals from the spiritual point of view, so we might well ask why not. The points I have raised are purely political or strategic, and they would not stand in the way if one were absolutely convinced of human spirituality as the route to wildlife preservation. Let's try to see, then, what it is about spirituality that has any relevance whatever to wildlife conservation. I will look at it under two categories.

NATURE IN THEOLOGY
This is not to be confused with "naturalism." There is little to be gained for wildlife by charging about the forest in beads and loincloths. Here I mean the role of nature and the nonhuman in the pervasive and important churches in our society. Apologists for each will no doubt produce reams of rationalizations to dispute me here, but I shall stand firm. I am particularly interested in the failure of organized religion to contribute one sausage's worth to the advancement of the cause of wildlife. On the surface of it, it does not make sense. Then again it does.

Many, including myself, have had things to say about the historic contribution of the Judaeo-Christian tradition to the estrangement of western man from his own biology, his alienation from his own being, and to the concreting of the notion of man's "dominion" over nature in the very foundations of western thought. This charge has been adequately borne out, and I do not intend to pursue it here. There are many sources in which you may trace the origins and evolution of the theological givens in our culture. Their effects have been catastrophic from a wildlife point of view. But all that is history, you could say, academic nitpicking. What about now? I shall address the now in the conviction that there has not been any perceptible shift in any branch of traditional western religion with respect to the relationship of man and nonhuman nature.

What interests me mostly here is the apparently wilful abdication of what I would perceive to be one of the prime roles of any church: to recognize the value to the human spirit of our life context. Nothing, it seems to me, could be more fundamental. If organized religions are to serve any purpose at all, surely it would be to purvey something of spiritual value here on Earth and now. What could be more appropriate for them than to attempt to understand the nature and spirit of *belonging*?

They are missing a heaven-sent opportunity, I think. Not only could they become "relevant" but also they might recapture their share of the market from some of the more zany persuasions that have drifted into the spiritual vacuum. Presumably it has not been possible for the churches to move with knowledge and philosophy through the last two hundred years because they have been unable to modify or temper or open their orthodoxies toward the acceptance of a universe that after all might not have been designed around man, nor indeed designed at all, a system that might not be hierarchic, a mode of interpretation that might not be dogmatic, nor even rational, a human being that might not be merely three-dimensional, a time that might not be linear, a cosmos that might not require causes, an order that might not be orderly.

You might well say that the influence of the established churches has been disintegrating for such a very long time that I am really setting up a non-issue here, stoning stained-glass windows, by suggesting the churches as serious factors in any sense. My feeling is that so long as cultural lip service continues to hold the churches in awe and respect, and so long as their world views continue to be the western world views, they are important. In spite of their apparent almost total inadequacy in "real life" issues, their past influence has been immense. (In some ways it still is; in redneck politics, for example.) Were the churches able to see and act upon the obvious as opposed to the theologically decreed needs of people, they might find a contributory role in society even yet, and might – just might – be of use to wildlife conservation.

Most naturalists tend to be pantheistic in mood if not in expression. There are no practising animists of my acquaintance, but there are few outright atheists either. There is, however, a deep and pervasive scepticism about institutions that pretend to hold answers or formulae for human problems while at the same time seeing man as outside biological process, and non-man as beyond the pale. On the other hand, there are a great many people like myself, who are waiting, with relatively open minds.

The shift in orthodoxy that would be required to make a church acceptable in the present day and in the present context would not be as radical as the bishops might fear. This is not a call for a crash program of arcane casuistry by the theologians, but rather a suggestion that there is an opportunity here to consider both the aesthetic and the ethical problems I have already outlined, on the basis of revelation well in hand. Man is a biologic being; a remarkable one, certainly, but still a biologic being, subject to the rules and regulations that apply to all beings in the biosphere, which is itself a biologic being. But there are opportunities as well as rules and regulations. These opportunities are lateral, however, not vertical; they are democratic, not theocratic; they are now, not in future; they are real, not mythic; they are individual, not institutional.

If it should turn out that the churches are in the business of *serving*, as opposed to protecting a vested interest in antiquarian antibiosis, they could yet be very positively important. If their call is indeed to serve man (or God), then their charge is to serve man and the environment from which he will always be inextricable. If, however, they persist in separating man from his living context, they can only exacerbate the contribution they have already made to the ecologic nightmare. (The technomachine is daily blessed by churchmen most high.) On the evidence, the likelihood of a change is not great. The likelihood of one coming soon enough to make any difference is even more remote.

Organized religion appears to have little or nothing to do with spirituality, which is after all an individual and not an institutional affair. It should be pointed out, however, that nature *does* have a role in theology. Nonhuman beings *do* have a role in the pursuit of inquiry into the natural history of God and other religious absolutes, if that is where your inclination takes you. I know of no formalized western theology, however, that even admits the kinds of questions that are raised by ecologic insight, much less begins to face them. The positive side of this is that ecologic insight gives rise to questions that require a spiritual investment for their open-minded pursuit that is qualitatively different from that dictated by any ecclesiastical dogma. It is much more difficult, but it is infinitely more rewarding, because it is about living. Living as experiencing is discussed in Chapter Four. Here let me merely say that I know of no even marginally useful argument for wildlife conservation that has been put forward by any of the major churches, and I can think of no honest argument that could be accommodated within their present positions.

NATURE "MYSTICISM"

Here we have a much more interesting issue, provided you do not read the word "mysticism" in any pejorative light. If you do, there is nothing to discuss. Mysticism has been around for as long as people have tried to label the kind of spiritual experience that is not satisfactorily explained either through approved orthodoxy or rational process. There are "religious" (here I mean truly spiritual) experiences that seem to arise out of individual intuition or contemplation, and that cannot be classified, labelled, and pigeon-holed. They occur in the quiet privacy of our minds. In others, we describe these experiences as "mystical," meaning "mysterious." We forget that there is no regulatory onus on the experiencer to explain his experience, nor even to discuss it. We also forget that such experience seems mysterious mostly because it cannot be force-fitted into convenient categories of common (shared) experience. Its whole reality is in one individual only. This the naturalist knows – profoundly.

There are all manner of posturers and charlatans who for various reasons like to advertise and even to preach their mystical experience. They may do this while assuming an aura of serenity that is meant to convey the message that they are privy to knowledge that is not ours. It should be obvious that the naturalist is anything but serene. Neither is he privy to the slightest scrap of conventional knowledge that is not available to all. His is nothing of the occult or arcane, nothing of the mystical.

There is however a very special, very personal, and at some times highly spiritual quality about the *experience* of the naturalist. He does not tend to advertise or proselytize the experience because of its intensely individual nature. But, paradoxically enough, he has an urge to transmit *something* to others. In its most developed form the urge is not to communicate fact but merely to share feeling. In a political sense it would be to the greater good were more people to partake of the experience, but in the glow of enthusiasm this, I feel sure, is not the motive. The joy is too great, too overwhelming, to contain, so it bubbles up. If you have not experienced it, you will have to take my word for it. If the naturalist does not know something you don't, he most certainly *experiences* something you don't. He is not serene. He is excited.

This experience defies communication and defies institutionalization and dogmatization. Since it cannot be rationalized and quantified, one cannot package it. Most especially, one can't politicize it. For this reason, I was one conservationist who was not especially happy when the "environmental movement," if I may call it that, was unilaterally adopted by the "counterculture" of the latter 1960's. This did wildlife preservation no good. Conservation in general tended to become identified with the attempts of the counterculture adherents to polarize opinion politically and otherwise on a wide range of issues. I believe that conservation, identified as it was with "environmentalism," was the loser in that instance, and it has taken it longer to become "respectable" again. To this day in the seats of power, which means in the corporate boardrooms and the highest echelons of government, "conservation" has too often meant "environmentalism" which has too often been interpreted as hippies and radicals intent on the indiscriminate overthrow of all things. This, whether we admit it to ourselves or not, it still a serious perceptual and thus operational problem.

This is not to downgrade the contribution of that period in history to general awareness of ecologic and related problems. However, as much of the credit does not belong with the "counterculture" as some have suggested. It had been coming for a very long time – since the 1930's really – and in the self-interest sphere, to be sure. What the counterculture did do was bring concerns of this kind to the attention of the young, who theretofore had been mostly absent from conservation councils. They still are. My regret is that the environmental concern was so often expressed in doctrinaire terms, as part of a larger ideological "package." It did wildlife little good.

Since much of the flavour surrounding the counterculture was selected from eastern cults, philosophies, and religions (somewhat indiscriminately, it seems to me), in more traditional eyes there was much of the "mystical" – again meaning "mysterious" – about it. (And in this case, "mystical" *did* become ever so slightly pejorative.) That there was spirituality there, at the individual level and at least sometimes, I grant. I do not however perceive that there was much in it of what I feel to be the spiritual experience of the naturalist. It was contemplative, to be sure, but it was inward. The universe of the counterculture was as homocentric as any designed in Athens or Rome. As it extended beyond the individual, it extended to other (human) individuals on a parallel "trip." Like most if not all romantic movements, it had little to do with living nonhuman nature. Its "environmental" aspect was social and cultural, not ecologic.

Lately, a useful distinction has been drawn between what are described as the "deep" and the "shallow" environmental movements. I would characterize the counterculture and much of contemporary "environmentalism" as the latter. The former is applied to the more reflective philosophic examinations of ecology and man, which although not the exclusive province of naturalists, tend to arise out of the naturalist's experience. Because the spiritual experience of the naturalist is so vividly personal and so resistant to classification and communication, there is small chance for us to "reduce" it to a form suitable for communication. This in spite of the long tradition of "nature writing" I mentioned earlier. There is much in our literature that persuades the reader very close to the qualitative experience of nature. Oddly enough, the best of it has not been written by "practising" naturalists, or at least not by people primarily known as naturalists. A Yeats, a Lawrence, a Coleridge, an Eliot, a Frost, or a Whitman–yes, a Poe–brings me ineffably closer to the core of *experience*–and thus of the nature of things–than most of the purple, adjectival, mawkish outpourings that I find on the "nature" shelves. That is because the best of them are talking about *nature*, not projected-reflected narcissism. About living in all of its dimensions. They are sometimes described as "mystical."

Mysticism is a private and individual experience. So too is the spiritual state of being that is wildlife preservation. It is not communicable in the usual ways because it cannot be presented through logical explication. It is non-argument, non-rationality, non-sense.

It seems to me that spirituality, whether in the form of traditional religions (western or eastern is of little consequence) or in that of individual "mystical" or intuitive experience, has not yet developed as a workable, reliable, or effective argument on behalf of wildlife preservation. That spirituality of some indefinable sort is close to the root of the naturalist's ethos is indisputable. We have not yet found a way to market it. We are not even certain whether we should try to market it.

The Central Assumptions

In all of our arguments for wildlife conservation there are certain basic assumptions. Some are stated; more are implicit. Since I am concerned with the *effectiveness* of our various arguments, at the risk of seeming repetitive, I want to do a brief review. It will begin to isolate and shed light on our assumptions. In many cases it is the assumptions themselves that ultimately determine the persuasiveness of our arguments.

Self-interest (prudence) assumes, essentially, that the human being is capable of acting in anticipation of things to come, of profiting by experience, of planning on the basis of knowledge of possible outcomes. This is the assumption that people will not rebuild their houses in the flood plain after the deluge, or that they will scrupulously save and invest now against unspecified future reward at an undetermined date. In brief, it is given that we are willing and able to act in our own future interest, even though the form of that future is by no means established.

It assumes further that wildlife conservation can be shown to be in the human interest. This argument requires the assumption of wildlife as a commodity that can be perpetuated in the service of man. Wildlife as a renewable asset assumes man as proprietor and decision-maker. An additional underlying assumption is that in each case a quantifiable payoff in cost-benefit terms can be demonstrated.

The human right of total access to wildlife for entirely human purposes is assumed throughout. Wildlife remains a human commodity whether man is principal or agent, emperor or steward. The utilitarian assumption runs through the entire roster of "wise use" arguments, and, albeit less visibly, in the "quality of life" appeal.

In the latter, the payoff is qualitative rather than quantitative, but there remains the assumption of wildlife as an asset in that man is the beneficiary whether or not he consumes wildlife on the spot. The investment metaphor holds, with the implicit assumption of right of proprietorship, even in the realm of aesthetics. Again, a future orientation assumes our willingness to pay now, benefit later.

The "ecocatastrophe" argument, the ultimate in the flood plain set of assumptions, assumes that you can actually scare people into acting in their self-interest, on, when it comes to wildlife, very flimsy evidence. The implication that wildlife can be shown to be in the human interest is rarely proven out.

Ethics as applied to wildlife assumes that a code of human intracultural behaviour in the social interest can be extended interspecifically. This assumes in turn not only interspecific reciprocity (which implies some mode of communication) but also that there is a wider social unit than man's, the members of which are able to act in the best interests of that unit. It assumes the human capacity to transcend the human interest and the nonhuman capacity to recognize not only its own but also the human interest.

In a very real sense the ethical argument requires that we see the nonhuman world in terms of the liberal egalitarian ideal: that the individual being is sacrosanct, that rights and concomitant duties, equitably proportioned, will serve the long-term higher purpose, and that "equity" can be applied to natural process. In brief, it anthropomorphizes the nonhuman world in order to include it in a human ethical code. All of this assumes an inter-species *summum bonum*; it assumes further that man, as proprietor, has both the right and the duty to *extend* an ethical code to those of lesser hierarchical standing.

It seems that arguments for wildlife conservation, whether couched in terms of human self-interest or in terms of human ethics, must either assume or result in a hard line of distinction between man and non-man. There appears to be the necessary setting up of a duality so that a "client" relationship may be perceived. There is the further assumption that people are able to see and act on behalf of future generations of people.

Spiritual arguments would like to remove the man/non-man distinctions, but those couched in theological terms can do nothing about the assumption of a man-centred universe. Although wildlife may be seen by the churchmen in an entirely benign way, man must be assumed as guardian or patron at the very least. God's steward on Earth enters into a landlord-tenant relationship with non-man. The assumed hierarchy is essential.

Mysticism, as we have seen, is an individual matter. Since there is no agreed-upon mystical argument for wildlife preservation, there are no prevailing assumptions.

Argument itself must assume communicability. Also it assumes logic, reasonableness, and persuasive evidence. It assumes dialogue.

Obviously, the difficulties raised by our assumptions are formidable. Whether tacit or acknowledged, they colour our entire process of reflection, and they cannot help but bring a fundamental bias to both our deliberations and our stated case for wildlife. Virtually all of our assumptions tend to reinforce and legitimize those concepts, so deep-rooted in our traditions, that have not only brought about the present condition of the life tapestry but also stand so implacably in the way of wildlife recovery. I should like to address some of those root problems directly.

CHAPTER THREE
The Root Problems

There is no assumption – just as there is no individual or species – that arises spontaneously out of nowhere. Like any other idea, an assumption, whether articulated or not, has an origin and an evolution and is able to persist at any given period only because the prevailing environmental climate permits it. Were it not "adapted" to the time and place, it would not be there.

In this chapter I look at some of the roots of those assumptions that seem to cloud our vision and inhibit our action in wildlife preservation. There are many of them, but they seem to coalesce into three general categories. There are those mechanical, operational, in-the-now problems that I shall characterize as "functional"; there are those that, arising from our social and cultural tradition, are ideal or "conceptual"; and there are those that spring from both our biology and our accumulated experience, and are in general "perceptual." All inter-relate and inter-act. Conceptual notions clearly help to shape both functional and perceptual difficulties, just as our perceptual capacities allow us to create and view both concepts and operations in certain ways.

The Functional Problems

The keystone of western civilization is the assumption of absolute truth. Our theologies, philosophies, science, and law, among other endeavours, require for their existence if not the tangible presence then the certain promise of unequivocally true answers. We behave "logically," under the over-riding assumption that just as there are reasons for all things, so all things – ultimate facts – are available to pure reason.

I shall return to this issue (which is of course a conceptual one) later, but I raise it here because it is at the heart of one of our most recalcitrant functional problems, and that is the matter of reasonable evidence. As we have seen, it bears heavily on the "ecocatastrophe" argument, and directly or indirectly on every aspect of the entire spectrum of "self-interest" appeals. In practice, of course, the usual absence of incontrovertible evidence is not a problem; the doctrine of "reasonable doubt" allows us plenty of freedom to leap to the conclusion that we favour. When it comes to the self-interest, especially if the argument is delivered in the form of a threat, nearly all of us want to be shown, beyond a shadow of a doubt. Ask any smoker.

The futurologists know better than the rest of us how extraordinarily difficult it is to convince the public or any significant part of it in the matter of futures that may be something less than appealing. As a result, most of them tend to bend, warp, or at least soften their predictions, or at the very least to leave available trap doors for the sweeping out of mind of any threatening implications.

Proving it in the case of wildlife conservation is not easy – in fact it is virtually impossible. (You should not be misled here, into concluding that wildlife plays any part whatever in technocratic planning and future-casting; I speak here of the futures outlined by ourselves, the conservationists.) Clearly we cannot *prove* anything in future, because the future has not yet happened. The best we have is hindsight reference to what has happened and is now happening around us. Unless there is a greater emotional investment in the future of wildlife than I can detect around me at the moment, mere uncertainty is a crashingly weak and insufficient argument. It leaves a gap of "reasonable doubt" big enough to drive the technomachine through. Even were there proof in hand, of course, we would have a perceptual problem, but that is another matter.

The unavailability of proof and thus of ultimate truth is a severe limitation to any conservation argument, but nowhere is it quite so bothersome as it is in the sorry burlesque that is "environmental impact assessment" from the ecologic point of view. I have already singled out this travesty for special mention; here we must attend to one special aspect of it. Now we are concerned with prediction. Many branches of science are quite comfortable with prediction (if they could not handle measurement, including extrapolation, they would not be sciences), but ecology is not in that position.

Although ecology has long since shed its swaddling clothes, it is still young and has much to learn. The more it learns the more it discovers that it does not know. In fact, "pure" (as opposed to "tame") ecologists claim to know only one thing for certain: that they will never know one thing for certain. I can think of no "hard" science so helplessly adrift on an endless sea of variables, their process relationships so complex that no individual mind can either encompass them or corral them for computer counting. Ecology does not know what its variables *are*, much less how to project them. When you remember that ecology is site- and situation-specific, forecasting becomes so vexatious that "ecologic prediction," though eminently useful jargon for the technocrats, is no more than a nonsensical contradiction in terms. Ecology cannot predict in the scientific sense; it can merely describe.

Historically, however, and for reasons which need not be elaborated in detail, wildlife conservation unfortunately found it necessary to accept the burden of proving the effect on wildlife and wildlands of various kinds of human activities. If the prediction could be quantitative, so much the better; all is possible in the rationalist-scientific world. Along the line it had become abundantly clear that there was little more than the most meagre constituency for "wildlife for its own sake" in the corridors of power, and rather than attempt to build that constituency whilst holding the philosophic line, conservation (at least in part for purposes of communication) chose to enter the mod arena of cost-benefit. That made us respectable. Now we could converse with civilized folk.

Thus the series of "self-interest" arguments came into being. If you won't save something for the sake of saving it, then here are some reasons. Unfortunately the juggernaut that is the current socio-economic order is fueled on hard data. Wildlife ecology just does not have them. All that an opponent in an impact hearing has to do is ask for conclusive evidence. More data. Like good little soldiers, we jump right back on the treadmill.

Having painted itself into a corner by attempting to quantify the human interest in species of wildlife, conservation desperately adopted the "ecocatastrophe" approach. Its effectiveness is well-known. When it accepts the burden of *proving*–of giving *evidence*–conservation effectively defeats itself. Having in mind the limits to ecologic prediction, wildlife conservation can never present an airtight case. And of course industry, commerce, and the growth imperative are required to *prove* nothing. Their goals are part of the belief system. Wildlife conservation is not.

There is another grave functional problem, also having to do with the future. Both the "stewardship" and "ethics" themes made specific reference to our duty to future generations. Other arguments contain the same injunction at least implicitly. There is an assumption: not only do we owe an obligation to the future, but also we are able to recognize and act upon our obligation to the future.

The fact seems to be that we have very great difficulty in entertaining any tangible feeling of responsibility for our descendants. I know that I can "identify," as they say, with my children, at least in the here and now, and for a stone's throw into the future. I am not at all confident that I can even *feel*, much less see, my way through their lifetimes. If I ever have grandchildren, I may be able to have a similar identification with them, but I will not be certain of that until I have seen and touched them. Certainly I cannot empathize with them now. (Indeed I feel much closer to the Peruvian cock-of-the-rock, a bird I have never seen in the wild, but that I know *exists*.) I am not at all confident, in other words, about my ability to feel any emotion at all in respect to future human generations, much less any responsibility. I think that this incapacity is not unique to me. I believe this is a true and real characteristic of all of us, no matter how often or how portentously we rhetorically indulge those not yet born.

I know very well that we *say* we can assume this obligation, but *can* we do it? I seriously doubt that as sentient beings we are really capable of abstracting that *idea* called "future" into a sufficiently palpable reality to allow us to accept responsibility of any serious kind. This is not meant as a criticism of our finer attributes; although I cannot prove it, it is a comment on something I suspect about our biology. Why, after all, *should* we be able to do it? "Future" will forever remain a concept, not a tangible; it cannot be an external stimulus, not ever.

Robert Heilbroner says it is "the absence of just such a bond with the future that casts doubt on the ability of nation-states or socio-economic orders to take now the measures needed to mitigate the problems of the future." I believe we have a major functional difficulty with this, not only as individuals but also as communities and societies and a culture. Although all sensitive folk castigated the senior publishing executive who asked, "What has posterity ever done for me?" I suspect he was more accurately interpreting the public pulse—the sociocultural heartbeat—than we do-gooders have been doing.

This brings us ultimately to that which is very probably the gravest of our functional problems, and that is the present (not the future) perceived self-interest of our society. I know of no argument for wildlife conservation that can so much as find itself on the agenda if the latter is cast in terms of contemporary human priorities. The poor are prevalent. I am not going to discuss the underprivileged overpopulated tropics and sub-tropics, because there seems simply no means of expecting a rational wildlife conservation argument there. (In such countries, by the way, the elites have no more interest in wildlife preservation than do the poor; it is not entirely a matter of economics.) In our own society there are also the poor; even more important is the industrial growth economy, which is not only a social phenomenon but also an article of faith. As long as profits must increase (who receives them is of no consequence here), and as long as yearly growth in the production and consumption of fabricated commodities is the sole measure of the health of a society, the blockade to wildlife conservation will be insuperable. There is little doubt as to which values come first, once things come to the "hard decision."

Functionally, then–which is to say in everyday practice– wildlife conservation arguments are expected to be expressed "rationally," quite in spite of (a) the limits to ecologic prediction; (b) the present locus of the burden of proof in such issues; (c) the apparent limits to effective human foresight and emotional commitment to the future; (d) the perceived socio-economic priorities of our society. I have not yet become quite so paranoid as to see this as a "conspiracy," but it has many of the earmarks. Let us merely say that it is one of those "Catch-22" situations that seem to emerge so predictably in virtually any aspect of the man-non-man relationship.

The functional problem, of course, turns out to be the belief system.

The Conceptual Problems

These have to do almost entirely with the western belief system. We live in a bottomless alphabet soup of givens and assumptions, and although each of us has his or her special little group of variances from the norm, relative to the whole they are small indeed. Outside the institutions for the insane, there are very few fundamental concepts that are not shared across society. Strange and wonderful though many of these may be, we can only touch on a handful. For example, there is no belief more basic than that concerning man's absolute power and authority over the non-human. As we have seen, from it have sprung most of the assumptions underlying our arguments for wildlife conservation.

A corollary of this is the belief that in the order of cosmic and Earth imperatives the continuity (immortality) of the human species has the ultimate priority *over all other things.*

Although it looks as preposterous as it properly should when you set it in type, the belief is very real. This conceptual precedence over nonhuman animate and inanimate "nature" is a cultural mutation, not a biologic one, and it has not necessarily been common to all human cultures. It so pervades recent and contemporary thought, however, and has become so concreted through generations of tradition, that it is almost as though it were genetic. It is as fundamental to the thinking of the "developed" world as the notion of linear time.

Quite simply put, the conceptual power structure consists of an imagined evolutionary hierarchy in the Aristotelian mode, with man as the apex of a pyramid, as the topmost growth bud of a tree, as (for modest men) the penultimate link in a grand chain leading from the dust to God. At progressive levels downward from our platform there are ranked and arranged those beings of "lower development." Thus a baboon is more "highly" evolved than an albatross, which is more "advanced" than a butterfly, which outranks any giant redwood. And so on, down the line.

The obsessive practice of ranking, grading, and assigning relative "worth" or "importance" to things (especially nonhuman things) is ancient. It is undertaken mainly, I think, in the interests of self-assurance. It is a most effective means of sustaining the conceptual power structure over the nonhuman. In another context it is sometimes known as the "kick-the-cat syndrome."

Evolutionary ranking through life continuity is justified on the assumption that evolution, up to the present time, has been purposeful, deterministic, and (most especially) progressive. And it is now *over.* Man is the final and only absolute parameter of evolution. All things were set in motion toward a single goal – the shaping of the ultimate creation, the Reflective One. Were the whole deliberate process to begin again, it would necessarily culminate in the same form. Evolution could have no other "purpose"; no other would make sense.

THE CONCEPT OF "MAN/NATURE"

The conceptual human power structure over nonhuman beings is supported and sustained by an even more radical belief, that of the fundamental difference between man and the nonhuman. Not just between man and chimp, or man and australopithecine, or man and bird, but the basic qualitative gulf between man and *all other sentient beings.* Man is in one compartment; all other life is in another. Our unshakable insistence on this has familiar manifestations. It is as though man were in some mysterious way abiotic, as though in some profound sense man were outside biologic and ecologic process. Thus we have "man *and* nature," "man *in* nature," "man *of* nature," "man *from* nature." The conjunction does not matter; the proposition is the same. The conceptual dualism is clear. Occasionally, in fits of desperate goodwill, we may substitute a slash "man/nature" in a well-meant attempt to indicate a bridging "interface" or ecotone, whilst all the time and often quite unwittingly underscoring the image of two discrete life systems.

Even when we do get around to acknowledging man as a biologic being, we appear to hold that he is quite a different *kind* of biologic being. Teilhard de Chardin, for example, seriously proposed man as a separate phylum from all the other chordates (animals with spinal cords). I am quite certain, however, that he saw man as outside the animal kingdom entirely. Thus we would have three life categories: plants, animals, man. Although we do not very often get around to pronouncing things like this out loud, in general, this is the way western culture sees it. In spite of our precious rational process and in spite of our cherished scientific objectivity, we continue to maintain an absolute and unchallengeable distinction between man and the nonhuman. It has occurred that the firmness of this insistence may be one measure of the need we may perceive for justification of our overwhelmingly antibiotic actions.

Life is filled with ironies, and I detect one here. There *may* be evidence to suggest that we *are* different not in degree but in kind. It arises from what would seem to be the uniquely human capacity to conceive of interspecies dominance hierarchy.

THE CONCEPT OF INTERSPECIES DOMINANCE

Many kinds of animals live in social groups; many do not. Leopards are "loners"; lions live in prides. Wolves have a very intricate and interesting social system, and so do some of our closer relatives such as chimpanzees and gorillas. In such groups, we see individuals occupying relatively stable social positions in relation to the others, in a kind of "peck order" such as is well-known in every henyard. This system of organization is called "dominance hierarchy." Those who have carefully observed the workings of such organizations in wild animals have emphasized the positive value of the arrangement. It is adaptive, survival-oriented. In other words, it works.

Hierarchy seems to work for the group because it is a manifestation of what is probably one of the most fundamental characteristics of life – the drive to co-operate (the "compulsion to comply"). I am trying not to be "mystical" in suggesting that after a lifetime spent in the appreciation of nature, the single factor that appears to me to be more important than any other is *compliance*. I can very comfortably interpret ecologic interdependence as co-operation. When a predator takes one of "my" grouse in the bush, it is not a crime against me or against God. It is co-operation on the part of the grouse. There is such co-operation, effectively, at every level of the ecologic structure. This is the point made earlier in the discussion of "rights."

Those species that live in groups achieve co-operation at least in part by a hierarchical structure in which the status of the individual has to do not only with other individuals but also with perquisites and responsibilities. Social status ("rank-order") in those species is essential not only for the survival of the individual but also of the group. For one thing, it does away with the inevitable quarrels and conflicts that would arise from a more "democratic" arrangement. Quarrelling and fighting waste energy, and also take your attention away from matters of security. Most important, though, a kind of ritualized or conventionalized social behaviour eliminates any need for jousting, which if carried to extremes has rock-bottom survival value. Food, shelter, and sex are all secondary imperatives; they are the rewards of social compliance.

Rank-order in nonhuman social groups is always in slow flux as those at the top age and drop away and young adults mature. Also – and this is important – groups tend to stay at about the same size. We cannot get into a discussion of the mechanisms that appear to regulate populations, but it seems that there are in each species upper limits to the size of group in which proper social organization can be maintained. This upper limit varies from place to place and from species to species, but organization is absolutely essential. Zoos have learned by sorry experience not to put too many baboons together, for example, in a confined space. The blood-letting can be severe – much as in human cities. Such behaviour does not have survival value.

The *pattern* of social organization is peculiar to the individual group. It has been worked out, as it were, by that group only, and every individual in that group knows his or her place in relation to every other individual. It does not extend to neighbouring groups, which have their own particular organization. Groups tend to keep away from each other, and when wandering individuals happen upon a strange group, there can be turmoil until the newcomer is accommodated (or rejected). Not only are social patterns specific to individual groups but also they are not extended to neighbouring groups of *other species*. That aberration is reserved for man: here, human uniqueness moves into sharp focus.

We have a remarkable tendency to perceive (believing is seeing) cross-species dominance hierarchy in other animals. Naturally it would be very satisfactory could we find a precedent in nonhuman nature. So, we observe interactions between individuals of different species and leap to the conclusion that some species are "dominant" over others. We are forever seeing "aggression" in nature; we like to read malevolence into the behaviour of a meat-eating predator, or belligerence into the behaviour of a grosbeak at a feeding tray. We forget that the predator and the seed-eater are merely feeding, and that feeding is basic and urgent.

Granted, we sometimes see birds of different species competing, as it were, for possession of a prized nesting-hole. This we swiftly transpose into interspecies aggression (striving for dominance), when what it really is, is competition for a nesting-hole. It would take the wildest foray of the human imagination to interpret it as illustrating an interspecies social dominance issue, complete with mutually understood rank. But we do it all the time.

Interspecies acceptance of social dominance hierarchy would be impossible, at least in part because the multitudinous species involved would not be able to understand each other's conventional symbols of rank: rituals, signs, language. A peacock displaying in front of a goose is going exactly nowhere. In the simplest terms, communication is generally understood as the transmission and reception of *mutually understood* signals. You have a sender and a receiver and a message understandable to both; otherwise you do not have communication. The dominance hierarchy in a group of social beings is based on a system of signs and signals which, whether the individuals learn them or are born with the knowledge or both, are usually fully understood and acted upon by all concerned.

On the other hand, the conceived human dominance hierarchy is completely one-sided. This is not communicated, because we are the only ones who understand the message. There is massive transmission, but no reception. Our physical power is so great, however, that, at least to our own satisfaction, we are able to display our dominance whether or not nonhuman beings "get the message." Thus we are able to fool ourselves as to our role. One of our prime self-delusions is that nonhuman nature *accepts* our dominion, as part of the natural order of things.

Before we go further with this, a word on how dominance hierarchy seems to work in nonhuman societies. We usually describe the top dog as "Alpha." There may be individual rank-order down from there, or there may not, depending upon the species and the situation. In any case, except for the inevitable turnover through time, one thing we consistently see in patterns of hierarchy is their stability. This homeostasis seems to be maintained, at least partly, by the way in which both dominant and submissive individuals behave. Their behaviour tends to reinforce their positions in the scheme of things. Sometimes you can recognize Alpha in a henyard or a baboon troop by his or her appearance, or posture, but sometimes not. Very often it is much easier to *infer* which individual is Alpha by watching how the *others* behave. The way the subordinates act can often direct you to an individual who does not appear to be doing much of anything at all. The others are behaving *in relation* to that individual, who turns out to be Alpha. Watch an individual back away from water or food, or step to one side on a trail. Then watch the other one. You have found Alpha.

It's rather like trying to spot the human Alpha in a large crowd. You do not usually identify the dominant individual by his own carriage, but rather by the running about and breathless bowing and scraping and general obsequious behaviour of the people swirling around him. From this, you *infer* his presence, and indeed his qualities. Think how often it is that we infer a social hierarchical position in someone, not by his show of power, but rather by the show of subservience in his followers. We see many more displays of deference and submissiveness than we ever do of naked strength. Alpha does not need to do very much when power is constantly reinforced by his subordinates. He may indeed have greatness thrust upon him. Such is the case with a king, and it is also the case with a male gorilla, whose sheer size makes it quite unnecessary for him to do anything at all. Also, lest we forget, there is no shred of evidence to show that either the king or the Alpha gorilla ever *wanted* to be where they are.

In the course of studying individual interactions between members of groups of social animals, various ethologists have called attention to what they have called "inhibitions" against fighting. At the approach of the biggest or "dominant" male wolf, for example, another individual may roll over on his back like a puppy, or slowly move his head to one side, making his throat openly vulnerable to the slashing fangs of the large male. But nothing happens. Many like to conclude that the big animal is "inhibited" against attacking; the action of the subservient individual prevents the attack. They say that he is "inhibited" because they apparently presuppose that the wolf is by nature a bloodthirsty, slavering killer, and has to be prevented from indulging his true "instincts."

This interpretation, like so many of our perceptions of nature, is the victim of our presuppositions about nature. No doubt it would be a wrench to have to abandon "nature red in tooth and claw," but that is where an unbiased appraisal of what we observe must lead us. I know of no evidence whatever to show that the wolf or any other animal, including man, is innately savage. The one characteristic that seems to cross all species borders is compliance. The big wolf does not need to be prevented from attacking; he has no intention of attacking. Both he and the subservient wolf are complying with the social imperative against internecine fighting. Indeed by going through this little ritual they are solidifying and reinforcing their particular social relationship. Nothing could be more destructive of the group integrity than to have one or more of its members injured or incapacitated when the time comes for feeding.

There can and will be fighting, however, when the appropriate signals of compliance are not forthcoming. In such cases Alpha appears to be triggered to action by some perception of disharmony (disorganization) which he swiftly moves to correct, in the group interest. It is true that there are occasional fights between apparently equally matched "dominant" males in non-human societies, but these are usually very short-lived, and, it seems, most often lead to early peace.

I am strongly persuaded to the view that in "real life," which is to say nonhuman nature, there is no such thing as dominance. Dominance may well be an inference to which we attribute reality, or, if you will, a human projection. It seems to me that what we anthropomorphically call "subservience" or "submissiveness" or even "obsequiousness," but what is in fact *compliance*, is the inherent drive that makes the biosphere go round.

If indeed "dominance" is manifested and hierarchy maintained at least as much by the actions of compliant individuals as by the actions of Alpha–perhaps more so–then the failure of nonhuman nature to receive our message of superiority, to accept our dominion, and to act accordingly creates a genuine problem. Here perhaps is a root cause of much of our cognitive dissonance with respect to wildlife. But since the one thing the Rational Being cannot do is leave the question open, we must *pretend* that nature is indeed complying, and is playing its proper reciprocal subservient role. And that is exactly what we do.

But it is one thing to pretend and another to make the pretence *rational*. We have a neat way of doing it. Since wildlife cannot or will not see us in a dominant light (we are not of their species, therefore we are socially irrelevant), all we have to do is see wildlife in a human light. Then everything falls into place. We do this by seeing wildlife *comparatively*. We judge wildlife species by human standards *in order to find them wanting in human qualities* so that they may be appropriately ranked and filed. Because our standards are specific to us, no other species can possibly meet them. Man is thus the rational measure of all things; the proof is universal, and the perceived hierarchy is firm. There is not a word of protest; we infer compliance. (Consider if you will the possible outcome were united gerbils of the world to declare gerbil qualities as standards for determining interspecies hierarchy. Perhaps indeed they have done so, and live in total comfort and assurance.)

It is essential for the interspecies dominant to cast other species in his own image, not to see himself in theirs. The beloved dog is "almost human." To anthropomorphize the nonhuman is much more salutary from an ego point of view than it would be to zoomorphize ourselves. After all, we are but one species and nature is millions; it is more satisfactory to assign roles to those bewildering multitudes in the monospecific human hierarchy. To attempt to do otherwise would be meaningless, because the only universal meaning is in human supremacy.

Thus it is that anthropomorphism becomes more than merely an irritating aspect of the Sunday supplements, the performing captive dolphin shows, and the "true-to-life" nature films. It is a fundamental need for the self-styled Alpha. Whether or not the concept is carried into action by way of overt force is incidental so long as "lesser" or "subhuman" beings are seen as appropriately subservient and submissive.

One of the more rewarding aspects of anthropomorphizing is that it allows us to attribute to other forms of life certain qualities and motives which, so far as one can tell, are uniquely human, and then to act accordingly. There appear to be "good" and "bad" human individuals; there must then be "good" and "bad" species. Once a human attribute has been assigned to a nonhuman being, it becomes possible to perceive that being as an errant human, and to take appropriate remedial measures. We can bring to bear all human ethics and law against the fox who "steals" a chicken. We can rename the orca "killer" whale and carry on in suitable fashion. To see the great horned owl as a "cannibal" and a "bloodthirsty murderer," as some of the nicest people have done, is to justify appropriate punishment. Conversely, the sweetness and light of the tranquil garden serve to reflect the poet's self-satisfaction. This is part of the same process. To cast the rest of nature in our image allows us to use human criteria in the valuation of the nonhuman, absolutely guaranteeing the perpetuation of the perceived scale of cosmic priorities. No shell game was ever more remorselessly rigged.

Anthropomorphism has a long, long history. On the record, as we have it, it turns up first in some of the scrawlings on cave walls that show creatures part human, part nonhuman. Later we have supernatural beings, and inevitably these begin to assume human form. Much later we have Mediterranean myths having to do with people in animal form, and so on. One anthropomorphic God turns up a bit later. Then it is on to stereotyping, various species being vested with sundry (human) attributes, which in turn allow the valuation of relative worth.

One of the very best examples of the uncanny way in which we can twist things around occurs in the present day. In describing the Alpha male of some primate societies, some anthropologists have gone so far as to call him the "despot" of that group, and to refer to social rank-order as "social despotism." The extraordinary thing is that this is nowhere visible; it is entirely inferred. Believing is seeing. The conceptual-perceptual overlays are interesting.

In practice, the function of the human despot has a special twist. In other group hierarchies, Alpha provides defence and reassurance, permission and protection. He carries out many important responsibilities; they sometimes cost him his life. The self-perceived human Alpha, on the other hand, persists in denying those in "lower" positions the largesse of his tenure. At the very least, he is imperially indifferent to the well-being of the infrastructure. He is the sole beneficiary of the organization. Again, the flow is one way. This, over the long term, does not have "survival value."

The survival value to the group (and thus, ultimately, to the species) of dominance hierarchies in nonhuman social beings is basic. A nonhuman Alpha who did not carry out his several obligations to the group would soon be selected out. Those dependent on him would no doubt be selected out also. This is to say that the survival value of a dominance structure that is incomplete (one way, non-reciprocal) must be severely limited. We like to forget this.

I am quite confident in surmising that one of the reasons that nonhuman beings do not accept our unilateral dominance position (whether or not they might otherwise interpret the message) is that they probably cannot *conceive* of interspecies rank-order. They cannot conceive of it because they don't need to be able to. They—especially those that are highly social—play out their individual lives within the internal structure of their individual groups. They do not appear to require the constant, repetitive reassurances that they might otherwise derive from projecting their own hierarchic structure onto neighbouring groups of their own species, or of other species. They are self-contained, mature, "adjusted." Nonhuman beings, so far as I can tell, are totally devoid of the gnawing ache of "group ambition," much less "species ambition." They appear to me to be whole.

Man appears to have a piece missing. Perhaps that piece was the price, paid long ago, for the uniquely human quality of ambitiousness. For in our species, the ambition of the individual becomes the ambition of the group, the tribe, the species as a whole. Interspecies dominance becomes global—becomes cosmic dominance. The drive toward Alphaness becomes a species imperative. Dominance becomes the reason for being.

THE CONCEPT OF HUMAN IMMORTALITY

I think it is permissible for us to speculate that nonhuman beings cannot conceive of either interspecies dominance (ambition) or of interspecies submission (fatalism) because they are not hagridden by our peculiar brand of fear. Man is the fearing animal, the anxious animal. Species ambition in man seems to be the inevitable consequence of fear, or, at the very least, of chronic insecurity. Anyone who requires reassurance in the continuing massive doses western man demands, would be said to have a problem. I believe we have a problem.

It is generally accepted that the most basic human fear is the fear of death. This may or may not be true of the individual, depending on his age, but it appears to be profoundly true of the species as a whole. If there is one single human imperative it is this: *man must not be subject to extinction*.

The very notion of extinction as applied to man is beyond decent consideration. I have found that the most shocking and offensive idea I can offer to my humanistic colleagues is that when man *does* become extinct, *he will never have existed*. There will be no one, no thing, on Earth to recognize our rubble for what it is, or to make any connection between it and anything that may have passed, so it will never be known that we were here. This, I am told, is the ultimate "pessimism"!

If I am right about the human immortality imperative, then human fear is the fear of natural selection: as individual, group, population, race, species. It is passing strange. In full knowledge of the splendid procession of diverse and beautiful forms which preceded us and now accompany us through Earth time, why should we fear to be part of it, I wonder? What is it that compels us to be first, I ask? What is it that impels us to be *last*?

It seems clear that our perceived dominance would be sorely affronted by an eventual turnover in Alpha incumbency. (That there must be an interspecies Alpha is given, it appears.) We believe that we are sufficiently in control of and qualitatively different from the natural infrastructure, that we quite clearly resent the possible application of life rules to ourselves. Since the goal and the purpose of evolution were to produce man, it would make no sense for the ultimate creation to thereupon become extinct. That would contradict the rationale for the entire life process. World without man is quite literally unthinkable.

Also, it would seem to be something less than fitting, proper, or appropriate that the stuff of a human being should undergo breakdown and subsequent recombination in the forms of sundry lesser organisms. Man clearly was meant for something more heroic than to be reprocessed through a series of plants and invertebrates, like some animal. Hence the steel-and-concrete mausoleum. Of necessity, man must persist, and in human form, for as long as there is Earth. There could be no other conceivable cosmology.

If, as I perceive it to be, species ambition is related to our morbid fear of selective pressure, then species ambition is also an important element in the continued maintenance of the conceived interspecies dominance hierarchy. If we must remain extant as a species at any cost, then no cost is too much to pay, even in the here and now, including the cost of our unilateral estrangement from nature and from life process. The double-bind is firm. The harder we struggle toward immortality, the fiercer becomes the suffocating vise of alienation. The conceptual man/nature dichotomy and the dominance structure, both spawned in our unprecedented self-conceit, are mutually reinforcing against the ultimate fear. Thus are we rendered immobile as sentient beings.

So it is that in practice – in everyday affairs – the fear is sealed off, closed out, denied. The sealants are freely offered by the humanistic tradition. Since our culture cannot admit even the faintest suggestion of the primal dread, only its substitute – the immortality imperative – remains. The conceptual surrogate becomes the reality. It follows that no new evidence, no new insight, no old memory, no heretical speculation can be admitted to question the conceptual interspecies rank-order. Human immortality depends on its safe-keeping.

It is the immortality imperative that, in an operational sense, effectively emasculates the "ecocatastrophe" and related long-term, self-interest arguments for wildlife preservation. Here again, although we can follow the conservation argument intellectually and rationally, there inevitably comes a point at which the conceptual portcullis thunders down and we once again find ourselves secure in the quiet dimness of shuttered minds. It's really quite simple. You cannot sow fear on ground that has been conditioned not to receive it. Our culture has seen to the conditioning. *What* fear?

Human immortality, which is a concept fabricated by our culture, turns out to be infinitely more potent than any argument of pure reason. Wildlife conservation, on the other hand, is *required* to be justified by pure reason, and cannot be. The fix is on.

If wildlife species are to become extinct, that will be regrettable. But any literate person knows that extinction is the way of evolution, and is in the fundamental flow of life. However, man is different. If man is not immortal, then there is no purpose or meaning in his existence. Which in turn would mean no purpose or meaning in the universe. The human immortality imperative is absolute and radical. That is why wildlife conservation has never been permitted to move to questions of ultimate value. There is no place for an ultimate nonhuman value in our western metaphysics, because *of necessity*, the human interest is the cosmic interest. That is what it is all about. Wildlife is an "externality."

THE CONCEPT OF HUMAN NECESSITY

The notion of necessity seems to underlie all but the most crackpot or subversive of our world views. Man is the Reasonable Being. It follows, necessarily, that the biosphere and planetary system of which he is part are explicable in reasonable terms. Since reason is based in orderly process, then it follows, as the night the day, that the cosmos is orderly. It follows still further that man is the necessary and inevitable product of that orderly cosmic process. And since man is the pinnacle of evolution, all activities that are in the human interest are by definition in the interest of the greater process.

Any observed phenomenon, whether man, animal, plant, or solar flare, or any other event, requires causes. There are reasons for all things, because all things are products of linear sequences of development toward assumed goals. It is a short hop from there to purposes, and from there to universal imperatives. If the highest purpose is the human purpose, then the purpose of the nonhuman is to serve that purpose, necessarily and inevitably. This is what we are saying every time we use the word "resource."

Causes, purposes, and imperatives are all subject to orderly classification and organization in a hierarchical system that illustrates the comparative value of a phenomenon (such as wildlife) in relation to usually undefined but assumed human ends. Certain of our assumptions, however, allow us to veer dangerously close to the final trap—the error of mistaking our own mental metaphors, symbols, and models for truth. The existence of absolute truth is of course the ultimate necessity, and the ultimate trap. I shall return to this.

None of this is to suggest that very many individual members of our species go about their daily business in constant preoccupation with matters of ultimate necessity and truth. Most of us do not. We don't have to; our most basic beliefs ("zero-order" assumptions) are taken as given. It is the unstated and unconscious assumption of these absolutes that influences virtually every human action with respect to the nonhuman, and even more important, shapes virtually every thought process having to do with the nonhuman portion of the biosphere.

The concept of necessity for our species could be illustrated in any of a number of ways, but appropriate for our purposes might be the hierarchy of human needs advanced by Abraham Maslow, since modified by others. I am taking liberties here with the original, but the sense remains. Progress through the steps is ascending, from the most fundamental (1) to the most exalted (5). In this case I would apply the scheme to humankind, not to the single individual, and as illustrative of the human necessity and the role of wildlife in meeting that necessity.

5. Self-actualization
4. Ego (self-esteem)
3. Social status ("belonging")
2. Physical security
1. Physiological base

Physiological Base
At the level of food and drink, there is little need for wild plants and animals in the human economy today, save for a very few isolated cases such as commercial fisheries, in which case the species concerned are seen not as wildlife but as a protein mine. Through the domestication of plants and animals (and of course ourselves) we have long since been freed from dependence on wild terrestrial species. Or so it is thought.

We tend to overlook the true extent of our dependence on wild nature, even today. We overlook, for example, the contributions of predatory insects in respect to agricultural "pests"; of nitrogen-fixing bacteria in the soils underlying our crops; of hawks, owls, foxes, and coyotes in rodent irruptions; of crabs and vultures and insects in sanitation; of mosquito-eating dragonflies; of water-purifying marshes, and so on. The list is not merely long; it is infinite. Nonetheless, from a conceptual point of view we are entirely emancipated from wild nature. The physiological base no longer requires wildlife, it is assumed.

If, however, some unplanned circumstance should arise to indicate that the physiological base requires the addition of new wildlife species—for whatever reason—the "knee-jerk" response is instantaneous. For example, the question of the propriety of killing dolphins in order to net tunafish can barely be articulated, much less addressed. The concept of necessity, so pervasive at so fundamental a level, precludes even the possibility of alternative perspectives, much less the formulation of questions. The role of wildlife at the human physiological support level is as basic and unquestioned as the sunrise, as unconscious as breathing. Far from being rooted in pure reason, the utilitarian role of wildlife is part of a giant autonomic nervous system that is shared by all mankind.

Wild plants and animals are *necessarily* the servants of man. How could it be otherwise?

Physical Security

Here the connection with wildlife is very tenuous indeed. Apart from those peoples who still use animal hides for clothing or shelter, the human need for security purposes quickly focuses on logs. Trees, of course, were set in place by an all-knowing providence for the purpose of supplying human dwellings. And if timber is needed – mostly, in our part of the world, for decorative purposes nowadays – that after all is what the forest is *for*. There are no doubts about that. Here, human requirements *of necessity* dictate the employment of the forest, and whether that forest contains orchids or woodland caribou or tapirs or orang-utans or indeed aboriginal people is quite incidental to the higher purpose.

In those unusual cases where a population of birds or mammals happens to be a reservoir of some disease (encephalitis, for example) that is transmissible to human beings, that reservoir must be eradicated. It would be unthinkable that there might be an alternative. My point here is not that such questions are never asked; it is that they can *not* be asked. They cannot even be framed. Questions outside the human interest do not exist, even in the most rational of minds.

Social Status ("Belonging")

Although it is clear that at least theoretically, realization of Maslow's entire ladder of needs is available to all, in practice we have difficulties at both individual and species levels. Rare, I believe, is the human individual in our society who is fully and comfortably at home in this category. It is a scarce commodity, "belonging," not in all human societies but certainly in our own.

I think that our pitiable failure here can be shown to be connected to our inability to understand the vital and radical importance of intragroup status or role in nonhuman societies. And of course our flat rejection of that biological imperative for social compliance that is ineradicably in our genes. This difficulty is impossible to overstate; it is of paramount importance, I think, in our relationships both with other human beings and with nonhuman nature. The denial of this part of our naturalness seems to me to have played an absolutely critical role in the process of our one-sided divorce, not only from nature but also from our own biology, and thus of course from our very selves.

I have pointed out that the most conspicuous and pervasive characteristic of nonhuman social organizations is compliance. Acceptance. Everyone in the social hierarchy knows his or her status or rank in relation to all the others. Notions such as status and rank are of course human concepts projected upon non-human systems. Here, we must drop the pejoratives and see merely "place." The notion of "rank-order" is misleading and I think destructive of our comprehension of what is going on. It is true that we can infer a hierarchical arrangement in that those close to the "top" defer to fewer and fewer other individuals, and Alpha defers to no one. What is really happening underneath all of this is that social organization is being maintained by means of unanimous compliance and co-operation, toward the general security and continuity.

You will be familiar with the ecologic model called the "food pyramid," the wide base of which contains millions of species of invertebrates, and the apex of which may represent only one species of "top carnivore," in a given locality. The pyramid represents not a reality but a process. It is a descriptive device, and a good one; it is easy to understand, and we all accept it. We seem to have difficulty, however, when we use the same device, essentially, to describe the social organization of nonhuman beings. The rabbit or the deer or the mouse or the big cat does not have a "rank" in the food pyramid, merely a *place*. Everyone does not *need* to be the final carnivore. Everyone does not *need* to be Alpha. One will do; there are other essential places to be filled.

Western culture notwithstanding, each of us does not in fact need to be Alpha. What we do need is a place, and any place will do, so long as we know it is ours. Then we belong. Then we have completed Maslow's level three. Relatively few of us achieve this level in the fullest sense, even though the drive to find an assured place seems to be one of the most insistent in our genetic inheritance. We are denied this accomplishment in a number of ways, and the denial festers in us. It manifests itself in all of the "antisocial" individual and group behaviour from high rise mayhem to war, with which we are too familiar.

I would suggest that sheer human density is the first of the several factors that contribute to this, the most brutal of all our problems. From a biological point of view, social organization appears to be impossible to maintain in a natural way (the way in which our genes demand it) at a population in excess of perhaps twenty-five to fifty. This would be the classic "extended family," and it would seem to be appropriate to both our social primateness and our social carnivorousness. In other words, our biology. This basic need is thwarted, swamped, repressed by our absolute numbers. For it we substitute such institutionalized organizational devices as ethics, religions, laws, politics, and many more, none of which, I would advance, is "natural" to us. Whether we realize it or not, and whether we acknowledge it or not, the frustration that results is grounded in our very being.

This is an enormously complex issue of which I pretend to understand very little, but of which I suspect much. Another factor is the competitive, goal- and achievement-oriented society in which we live. I can think of no aspect of our culture so destructive to children, and thus to the society itself. Instead of raising gimlet-eyed little achievers we might try our hand at raising little social beings. I suppose there is a Richard Nixon in every four-year-old, if we foster it, but so is there a compliant, co-operative, social creature who will accept any other social creature in peaceful relationship without hangups about "rank." He will know his place, given the opportunity to flow with his own biology, and he will be content. Not, I fear, in overpopulated, overmanaged, overinstitutionalized, overcompetitive contemporary society.

So it is that with social *place* denied to us we strive instead for social *rank*, and that not being available to all, we substitute commodities, "status symbols" of all kinds, including bizarre "life-styles," and all the other contrived and fabricated appurtenances of the craziness that is high civilization. Very few of us—an enviable, peaceful few—are able to break out of our cultural conditioning even sufficiently far as to see the problem for what it is, much less to achieve a stable place for a lifetime. (As one individual, I am only able to accomplish this prodigious feat rarely and for brief periods, but I think I can feel what freedom must be like.)

I find it deeply and sadly ironic that the most numerous large mammal on Earth, and in some ways the most successful that has ever existed, is so pathetically lonely and alien, even with respect to his own kind. The implications of all this for other, nonhuman biologic beings are obvious.

The *necessity* of striving for Alphaness in human society arises both from our biology (the frustration of the need for "place") and from our culture (ambition, competition, achievement). As I have pointed out earlier, we also have the conceptual necessity having to do with human imperialism over the nonhuman.

As a species, our sense of belonging in nature, our sense of a place in nature, has been utterly destroyed. The concepts of "man/nature," the drive toward interspecies dominance, and the human immortality imperative have seen to that. This is the unilateral divorce from life and living that is the unique accomplishment of our civilization.

Having wilfully abdicated our place in life process, we can no longer remember that "place" means "belonging," and that belonging is what living is all about. Since we can no longer conceive of a natural system that includes us, we feel estranged, alien, even resentful. Our bewilderment can turn ugly. This of course *is* the necessary outcome of our conscious and deliberate denial of nature, our nature, our life sphere. From this springs the paranoia that is the hallmark of every thought and action with respect to those aspects of nonhuman nature (weather, disease, death, rose aphids) not yet brought under our absolute control. We remain at level two.

Ego (Self-esteem)

When it comes to self-esteem, the alien is in bad shape. Solitude can weigh heavily on the self-image. Nothing can exist without a context; the context in which we now live, however, is one of our own imaginative creation. In spite of our posturing, it does not and cannot satisfy us as sentient beings. So it is that the self-image of mankind is in parlous condition, notwithstanding our protestations to the contrary. Our defensive attitude and actions toward nature are ample evidence of that, as is our problem with rank.

To me, it all seems very simple. So long as we are *necessarily* qualitatively different from, superior to, and exempt from natural processes—from our own being—the paranoia will necessarily follow. For the technosociety that cannot find a place at level three, self-esteem lies beyond comprehension.

Self-actualization

This highest level in the hierarchy of human needs is sometimes called "self-realization." Whatever either term really means, one would assume that is a purely individual affair. If it means becoming the fullest being of which one is capable, having in mind both nature and nurture, then you could say that in the absence of a standard the notion is meaningless or impossible, or you could say that by the mere fact of having lived, everyone achieved just that—everything of which he was capable. I do not know that. But I think I know that total achievement of the human "potential" (whatever that may be), whether for the individual or the collective, will not be possible outside our biologic context.

It is assumed in the Maslowian hierarchy that one must move through the levels in sequence, beginning with the physiological essentials, through physical security, and so on. If the abandonment of our own life context will not permit us so much as to reach a state of "belongingness" and thus of "self-esteeming," then it would seem that actualization for the alien species would be supremely difficult. We would need, for the process to complete itself, a relationship with the nonhuman which our culture cannot accept.

My own interpretation of "self-actualization" is death and recycling. I think the supreme achievement would be conscious abandonment of "self," and the sensation of release from life-long mental slavery, the joyful feeling of rejoining that very old and yet immediate familiar, the all-encompassing and all-receiving life process. At this point one knows "compliance." Having found it, one knows at last what had been forgotten, and what every nonhuman being knows with its every breath and every pulse, and in every cell.

Self-actualization for our species is, I fear, distant. It would require our acknowledgement of belonging in nature, our development of actual (as opposed to artificially conditioned) self-respect as sentient beings, and it would require open acceptance from the inside out. Not, I fear, just yet.

Our failure to see ourselves as and thus to again become an integrated functioning species in a dynamic context, and our inability to move past that point, arise entirely–it seems to me–out of the concept of human necessity. None of our most bizarre conceptual fabrications has had such far-reaching consequences for us, and thus for all of nature.

THE CONCEPTUAL HERITAGE
Our cultural tradition–the set of "givens" which engender, nourish, and shape both our attitudes toward nature and our overt actions with respect to nature–is a complex of concepts so deeply held that in practice it is rare even to acknowledge their existence much less to attempt to evaluate their effects. Here I have called attention to only a very few of them, but they are among those that I believe to be at the root of our difficulties in entertaining the very *notion* of wildlife preservation, much less implementing it in practice.

The conceptual qualitative separation from nature, the imagined human dominance over the nonhuman, the imperative immortality of the human species, and the notion of necessary human directions, goals, purposes, and reasons in the universe are of bedrock importance to all that grows out of them. They dictate not only how we frame the argument for wildlife preservation, but also how we fundamentally *perceive* wildlife, ourselves, and life process.

The Perceptual Problems

Our concepts – our ideas, thoughts, notions – about ourselves and the world around us both create and are created by our perceptions. As human beings, which is to say, primates, our sensory apparatus is heavily biased toward the visual. Thus we have "views" about ourselves and the biosphere; we "see" these phenomena in certain ways. Were we dolphins, no doubt we would have "sounds" or "echoes" about things; were we moths, we would forever be trying to make "scents" of things.

The handful of concepts I chose for attention in the preceding section all have close relationships with our perceptual activity. In fact, those relationships are as intimate as those in any ecosystem, with feedback mechanisms so complex and subtle that they relegate the chicken-and-egg problem to primer level. So interwoven are the dynamics of perceiving and conceiving that simple cause-effect labels and descriptions are worse than useless. They are downright misleading. In full knowledge of this, however, we continue in our stubborn positing of universal causes and effects, laws, reasons, beginnings and ends, one-to-one relationships, special status, and the mechanical explicability of all things. I often think that the most noteworthy characteristic of the Reasoning Being is his immunity to reasonableness.

This is not an essay in perception, but I must indicate my ground rules before proceeding to our perceptual problems with wildlife and its preservation. Perception has many definitions; the one I shall use here is "a hypothesis of the world based on sensory information." We are forever testing our hypotheses, matching internal "realities" against external ones, testing our inner worlds, which are always changing, against the "real" world. I see this constant process of change (growth, development) as necessarily including the process of identification – sorting out and identifying the sources of information that we receive through the five standard sets of sensory apparatus. We smell steak, we hear thunder, we feel sunburn, we taste whiskey-soda, we see the sunset. And of course we can do all of them at once. All of these sensory experiences are perceptions.

Always, in perception, there is much *imaging* going on. There is much picturing. As a continuing process of hypothesis testing, including identification, perceiving involves the *matching* of external stimuli with some internal image. If we did not know what we were sensing, at least most of the time, we would not be able to function at all. If I say "Red," you will instantly produce an internal image of red, but probably not the one I have in mind. If I now say "Rose-red," your internal image will be closer to mine.

Most of the time this process of internal imaging is the next thing to instantaneous. What we actually seem to be doing is *testing* a sensory impression (sight, sound) against a stored inventory of prior experience of that impression, which results in a match, an identification. It is like looking up the bird or the flower in your field guide. If, when you are walking through the apartment corridor, you don't happen to have on file the sensory experience of corned beef and cabbage, you cannot make a match, and you won't know what it is that so massively surrounds you. Or, if the experience in store doesn't *quite* match the smell, you can always force-fit pigs' hocks and sauerkraut. Force-fitting is a major perceptual problem.

I have a little image of my own that helps me to understand this process of perceiving. Picture inside your head one of those circular wheel-like file-card holders that you can rotate. You spin it around until you find the proper place, then stop it and read the appropriate card. It's like that. Each of our heads contains one of these devices, filled with cards, spinning around perpetually. When we receive a sensory signal of some kind, the wheel stops spinning, and up pops a little bubblegum card—what I call an image-card. That's what happened when I said "Red" and when I said, "Rose-red." No library cross-referencing system was ever so efficient.

We have to remember that one-to-one matches are not the rule. It's more complicated than that; no library has just one entry under each heading. There are many. So it is with our own filing systems. Sometimes it may take half a dozen or more cards to make even an approximate match. But we do the best we can.

Seen in this way, each image match is an event. Although perception is a constant and continuing process, it is made up of a series of countless discrete little matches, all of them part of the greater sensory perception process. Each time we make a match, the wheel stops (the world does not, and that is another problem). An individual perception is an event. "Red" is history; now you perceive "Blue." It is very much like a motion picture film, a series of individual frames. Each individual frame, in isolation, is soft and poorly defined, as the result of having been exposed while moving, and at slow shutter speed. A single frame from a piece of film is not satisfactory viewing. But strung together and projected at proper speed, that series of quite poor photographs at once becomes sharp and crisp and focused – the greater context. All of which is a way of saying that in spite of reductionist science, the fragments give precious few clues as to the nature of the whole.

In this world, at least, all things seem to be finite. For most of us, there appears to be a limit to the number of image-cards that we can accommodate in our little whirlygigs at any one time. There can be an immense number of them – and there is – but there is still a limit. Not an absolute limit in a biological sense, but a limit to what our culture is capable of imprinting upon us. It follows from this that everything – literally everything – hinges on what image-cards happen to be available at a given moment. Granted, we do shuffle them constantly as the consequence of simply being awake and moving; we sort and re-sort, tossing out old and inserting new, but at any instant we are limited in our perception to whatever image-cards happen to be in inventory at that instant.

Naturally, a problem emerges straightaway. Suppose whatever happens to be on file turns out to be out-of-date, or printed off-register, or upside-down, or badly translated, or wrongly filed – or indeed there is nothing there at all with which to match the next sense impression that comes in? You can see how some spectacular mis-identifications can occur. Misinterpretations. Misunderstandings. But of course – and here is the *real* problem – we have no alternative but to believe these matches to be accurate. Seeing is believing.

I happen to be a birdwatcher, and all birdwatchers treasure their skill, knowledge, and their virtuosity. In fact, many of us compete overtly and outrageously in the swiftness of our card sorting and the size of our inventories. Suppose I am sitting at my desk, and some faint bird song drifts down to me from the big shade trees outside. Now, I have stashed away a goodly number of image-cards representing birds of which I have had prior experience or I have copied from the texts. First, some mechanism that is so swift as to appear automatic, sorts the file geographically and comes up with the batch for southern Ontario. Then I proceed to match the sensory impression (sound) against that local batch, and out of the pile falls a bubblegum card, in full colour, of an American robin. I perceive an American robin, having had an image of one with which to match my sensory impression. Not any other kind of robin, of which there are many, but *that* one.

But, God help me (and my reputation), what if the filing system comes up with an image not of a robin but of something else; something that sounds a bit like a robin, but is not one? Perhaps a rose-breasted grosbeak. In that case, I'm in trouble, and my bird identification will be wrong, but I won't *know* that it's wrong. So how can I go about distinguishing between an accurate picture and an inaccurate one? They are both real, to me, and that is all that matters. They are both images, both in inventory. How do I choose?

Naturally there is always the possibility that I may have no image-card at all with which to even try to make a match. This happens regularly when I travel in unfamiliar places. In such cases, I simply will never know, and I will have missed a particular experience. This is one of our most radical perceptual problems. We are stuck with the image-cards we have – and only those – but sensory impressions are continuous and all-pervasive; we cannot shut them out. All we can do is *try* to make a match, and the margin for error is high. In fact, if you allow yourself to brood about it for a while, this potential for error becomes quite alarming.

Any aggregate of people – a cult, a community, a society, a culture – has a collection of image-cards that most if not all of its members share in common. When I say "Santa Claus" most North American readers will retrieve essentially similar image-cards. An Inuit or a bushman or a Chinese draws a blank. Most Europeans would display consistent images, but they would be a bit different from the North American ones. On either side of the Atlantic, however, there would be indignation and outrage were Santa to appear in a Batman suit. There is a vested interest in our images, and it is strong. I would refer you only to the image of human dominance over nature, for one example.

Each society has an inventory of images that is shared by nearly everyone. In each society, we have not only shared trees and colours and birds and folk heroes, but also we have shared ethics, theologies, philosophies, science, imaginative literature, music, graphic arts, aesthetics, beliefs, and assumptions. Remember that these image-cards are put in place by experience. Societies have experiences such as Santa Claus that are shared right across the board. Such too as nonhuman nature.

Another dimension to all of this is that while we share cultur-ally processed images we also share a common store of *probabili-ties* about the likelihood of such-and-such a thing being the case in such-and-such a set of circumstances. If the man far down below me in the street has got his umbrella up, then it is probably raining. If I see a little fluttering group of ivory gulls at the edge of the arctic ice-pack, there is probably a polar bear around. And so on. I will *probably* get my bird song right after all, because I have in reserve an approximation of the odds on the presence of vari-ous bird species around my house.

Notions of probability can be set in place either by personal experience or by cultural conditioning—usually a bit of both. I can read the geographic distributions of the birds in a book or several books, or I can learn them the hard way, by working them out for myself, in the field. Generally I will tend to accept the literature, especially in some "new" environment.

Our notions of probability are almost entirely subjective (we very rarely go around objectively estimating the odds on the sun-rise, for example). We accept them as given. Givens are *cultural* image-cards, and it is against these that I weigh, sift, filter, and attempt to match the various sensory impressions from the out-side to which I am exposed continually. It is through these givens that I perceive. My culture fits me with a set of pre-ground goggles through which to receive the world.

To be alive is to be experiencing a perpetual barrage of sensory impressions—sights, sounds, smells, and all the rest of it. In fact, in order to make living bearable, we have the facility to screen out or ignore much of that barrage from minute to minute, and to concentrate on particular portions of what is available. You screen out the barking dog, the screaming infant, the overflying aircraft, and at least occasionally the voices of those nearest and dearest. Your eyes can concentrate on the bird while dropping the bush into limbo. You can tune in to the voice of a conversational partner no matter how many conversations may be hububbing around you. You will pick up the scent of smoke no matter how many other odours may be swirling about the kitchen. This is a matter of some in-built capacity to select our impressions and also to lessen the potentially distracting or even maddening effect were all receptors to be left open to their fullest extent at all times. It's an unconscious protective mechanism.

There are times, of course, when we consciously reduce the barrage of sensory stimulation, as when in self-defence we take the telephone off the hook, turn off the radio, shut the window and door and try to get on with a backlog of homework. Then, we are consciously simplifying the sensory environment in order to concentrate as fully as possible on the task at hand.

There are still other times, however, when our sensory impressions are *severely* diminished, as for example when we enter virtually any contemporary institutional building, office complex or apartment high rise. Then we encounter the phenomenon known as sensory deprivation. In sensory deprivation, we are told, the victim experiences not lessened but *increased* imagery. He does not however experience perception as I am interpreting it here. Apparently what happens is this: the increased internal imagery is the result of the perceptual apparatus trying to keep going in spite of reduced or almost totally absent external stimulation. The little rotating wheel keeps spinning madly along, throwing up one image-card after another—including, it is said, many rarely used in usual circumstances—as though trying to find *some* external stimulus with which to make a match. It throws up card after card after card, wanting and trying in every conceivable way to keep in touch with the outside. But there is nothing coming in, nothing to match with, and the internal images are therefore meaningless. There is nothing. And of course we can never have an image-card with which to match nothingness because we have never experienced nothingness. We cannot experience nothingness because our culture cannot *accept* nothingness. So the wheel of sensory misfortune spins, and keeps spinning.

It is at this point that I advance my thesis with respect to the sensorily deprived society. I believe we live in a society of sensory deprivation, with all of the bizarre imaging that that implies. Now, whenever I put this notion forward in a lecture or some other forum, I am immediately pounced upon by the urbanists, who gleefully point out that I am obviously alone in an echo chamber of my own creation, because everybody knows about the painfully obvious urban phenomenon known as sensory *overload*.

Everyone knows that, far from being sensorily deprived, the average city dweller is fairly overwhelmed by a shattering and inescapable barrage of sense impressions—flashing signs, screaming horns, choking exhausts, bellowing shills, and all the rest of it—kaleidoscopes and cacophonies of every conceivable kind. Bumping, jostling, sweating, swearing humanity. And all of that is true. Certainly, in the city we are grievously and continually assaulted, and we defend ourselves by screening out that which we cannot or do not wish to assimilate.

But there is more to it than that. I believe that this urban sensory assault and battery, if we feel we must describe it as overload, is a simple quantitative overload, having no variety whatever. The tumult and the sensory hammering all come from one single source; without exception they are of human manufacture. All of our sensory bruises are self-inflicted. And when at last the tumult and the bombardment abate, we are left with the only monotonous landscape on Earth – the human landscape. Monotony is a prime contributor to the symptoms of sensory deprivation.

In a qualitative sense, far from being sensorily overwhelmed, we are virtually starving for variety. Something, anything, that is not of human manufacture, human fabrication. I can conceive of no other situation in which sensate beings are harshly and uninterruptedly imprisoned in this way, exposed entirely to sensory stimuli from a single source – themselves.

This is very sad, and I think very serious, because the problem feeds and compounds upon itself. In sheer physical retreat from the constant, terrible insults to our delicate sense organs, we tend to narrow even further the range of stimuli that we allow ourselves to receive. We find ourselves walking about in an even narrower prison of our own personal making, in sheer self-defence. Thus, whilst reducing the absolute quantity of the barrage, we reduce still further the range of potential variety. We reduce still further our own access to possible qualitative experience.

As indicated earlier, I see "quality of life" as the care and maintenance of options. I believe that *sensory* options – textures, scents, tastes, pictures, sounds – are the most fundamental and necessary of options, and those that we most consistently and perversely deny ourselves. This, essentially, is what I mean by sensory deprivation in civilized society.

I am trying very consciously not to be "romantic" about all this. I am not, by the way, a subscriber to the "wilderness mystique" and all of that. I mean, quite simply, that we very deliberately deny ourselves sensory access to the radical nature of being.

Thus it is that we find ourselves estranged not only from the life context external to ourselves, but also from our own being. *We are all alone.* No wonder we behave the way we do. Strange things happen in solitary confinement, and strange things happen too in high-density confinement. Paradoxically, the individual finds himself in high-density "solitary."

Incidentally, like others who have thought about this problem, I am surprised not so much by the high level of crime and other madnesses in our cities, but rather by the relatively *low* level of it, having in mind the appallingly deprived and degraded circumstances in which, as sentient beings, most of us live. From this point of view, I think, mankind may be even more admirable than the most zealously dedicated of the urban humanists have yet imagined. I can think of no other large mammal that would tolerate it. The blood would run freely in the gutters *every* night — not just on week-ends.

I think also that the extraordinary boom in the house plant business these days is a very good indication of a fundamental urban problem. I do not see it so much as a decorative fad as the expression of a deep and primal need – a biological imperative. To be alive means to be sensate means to be *in touch*. We have to maintain contact with something – anything – that is *alive*. It's the most fundamental part of being. The geranium on the tenement windowsill is both an offering to the mysterious tidal pull of some distant biological memory, and a heartbreaking cry for help.

Assuming as I do that this quantitative sensory barrage coupled with qualitative sensory undernutrition adds up to sensory deprivation of a very real kind, some of our most peculiar behaviour seems to make a little more sense. Like that of the experimental volunteer shut up in the soundless empty room, our internal perceptual machinery keeps throwing up its little images in its search for matching sensory impressions that are not there. It follows that as a society or a culture we experience a series of quite meaningless pictures: hallucinations, illusions. This I believe to be the common perceptual experience of the sensorily deprived society.

This society is of course the spawn of its environment (the interaction of its culture and itself). Our present predicament has entirely cultural roots. The tradition out of which we have come has, by a process of artificial selection as sophisticated and complex as that of any geneticist, produced a cultivar so remote from its origins that they are barely discernible. We have been unceremoniously ripped from our life context, sprayed in plastic, and packaged in hermetically sealed containers. Sealed off from our own aliveness, including our sensory processes. All this has been done through cultural conditioning. We have been divorced for so long not only from biophysical nature but also from the very *awareness* of biophysical nature that our images of the world and even of ourselves have become little more than institutionalized hallucinations.

Our culture has institutionalized such hallucinatory images as human supremacy over all animate and inanimate nature; a swollen, obese GNP as the very model of social health; high technology as the Holy Grail, and so on. There is even a picture of a planned, organized, ordered, and thus understandable and manageable universe. The trouble with all of these counterfeit bubblegum cards is that there is no external "real world" opposite number with which to match them. They are displayed into emptiness; they are without meaning. They are, in my view, precisely the sorts of hallucinations that arise in sensory deprivation, in the absence of natural sensory stimuli. If perceiving really is hypothesis testing, then many of our most treasured hypotheses are not testing out.

So it is, I think, that our perceptions (and our concepts) having to do with man and nature and the cosmos, are images that reflect the "real thing" about as accurately as toy poodles with painted claws resemble the wolf, as assembly-line leghorns resemble the red jungle fowl, as glazed castrated Herefords swimming in drugs resemble the great white aurochs. The image no longer matches the reality. Our culture sees to it that sensory impressions from the natural world are consistently screened from us, so that both as individuals and as societies we are permitted to perceive only distorted images of our own queer, tortured, internal fabrication.

In this sense our hallucinations about the relationship between man and non-man, for example, become understandable. By closing off our connections with external reality, which happens to be our root system, our culture drives us to dependence on entirely artificial support. We are left with a jumbled catch-bag of monstrous illusions, and what is more, we take our hallucinations for truth. Seeing is believing. Even more important, believing is seeing.

The gestalt psychologists explain many of our problems in terms of what they call "closure"—sealing off potential sensory impressions (or ideas) which might otherwise rock the boat, simply by penetrating the human consciousness. This must be avoided at any cost. After all, my personal set of institutionalized beliefs is complete and finite. So is my society's. Don't intrude. Don't annoy me with facts. Closure is described as the attempt to see all things as neat and orderly and symmetrical, and to ignore holes or anomalies. We want to see everything (including ourselves) nicely and evenly balanced; we want an idealized perfection. We feel secure that way. (Professional proof-reading is often given as an example of what closure is *not*. Most of us make terrible proof-readers because we read for content, and close out the typographical errors. We never see them.)

But any naturalist should know that there is no security, nor any beauty, in symmetrical, balanced order. The birdwatcher looks for differences, not similarities. Two things the conceptual ecologic model does not demonstrate are symmetry and balance. If it were to exist, symmetry would indeed be fearful. The hoary old "balance of nature" image-card does not imply a static, controlled state of affairs. The so-called balance swings and yaws and bumps and pitches quite asymmetrically around an hypothesized homeostatic line. But homeostasis is never achieved. If it were, everything would thereupon lock and stall. Stalling is not what life is all about.

Unfortunately, our western institutionalized perceiving seems to be predisposed to cleave to the hallucinatory image of balanced symmetry, which is a life contradiction. Nonetheless, the drive is very real, a kind of cultural imperative. This appears to be manifest in the urge to reduce perceived "chaos" or disorder (which is bad) to manageable and controllable order (which is good). Unfortunately for all of us living sentient beings, the human assumption of the possibility – no, the necessity – of perfect balance and symmetry, whether in the individual, the society, the landscape, the biosphere, or the cosmos, looms very large as a potentially disastrous self-delusion. Such a belief, when force-fitted to outside stimuli, can result in some very strange misinterpretations, which in turn may be seen as indivisible and absolute cosmic truths.

Predisposition is exemplified in "optical illusion" drawings, especially those at which you may have three alternative ways of looking – a choice of perspectives. You can see only one perspective at a time, because that is all your brain can handle. Once you have made your first impression, however, you tend to "lock" into it, and it can be difficult to switch off that (acquired) predisposition to see the same picture from a new perspective. This is the way, also, with cultural predisposition.

From the point of view of wildlife preservation, our western perceptual predispositions are clearly and sadly illustrated. Such is our cultural image-making apparatus that it is the next thing to impossible for us even to *perceive* wild plants and animals as anything other than human amenities, utilities, or commodities. The humanistic tradition has done its work so well that it is the next thing to impossible to perceive any arrangement other than a man-centred and man-dominated universe, any purpose other than the human purpose, any process that was not designed for the exclusive benefit of man. It is next to impossible for anyone, however highly motivated, to see wild plants and animals as more than man's wards, "incompetents" in our custodianship.

Thus it is that the less well-motivated, and the less-informed, see natural predation as murder, tunafish as a gold mine, dead porpoises as externalities, human mortality as unnatural, wild nature as alien and hostile enemy. The roots are long, and deep. They nourish and produce not only our arguments for wildlife conservation, not merely our assumptions, not merely our concepts, but also our very perceptions of that life tapestry of which man is but one part in millions.

I believe that we are what we perceive, no more – and no less. This is not meant to be a value statement; it is a descriptive statement. I have been a naturalist and preservationist for over forty years. If you are not a naturalist, then I have perceived more widely than you have, and I have experienced more widely than you have. (This is not meant to sound presumptuous; if your experience, however rich, has been entirely in the human context, then mine has been richer.) I do not attach any "value" to this in a comparative way, because the only value has been for *me*. I know that I perceive differently than the non-naturalist perceives not merely in knowing the labels for the biophysical surrounding and its parts, and in being able to understand some of its process. The fundamental difference is that I *feel* (sense, apprehend, conceive, perceive, experience) them differently than the non-naturalist does.

This is not an attempt to turn you into a naturalist if you are not already one. To be perfectly frank, I have no emotional investment whatever in the expansion or the constriction of your experience. I am no more than human; I don't know you and I cannot "relate" to you or to your emotional or intellectual welfare. What I *do* care about, of course, is the way in which your perceptions of yourself and of nature may influence your actions with respect to wildlife preservation. And that's *all* I care about. But in my universe, that's everything.

And so it becomes blindingly apparent to me that it is in my interest to talk about your interest. If you were to become a naturalist, I would be the beneficiary. Your becoming a naturalist would further my investment in wildlife preservation. This argument is not addressed to your self-interest in wildlife (whether for altruistic or consumptive reasons); nor even, as an argument, to the interest of wildlife as such. It is in *my* interest.

This is where we join hands. There is no interest but mine – and yours. There is no *reason* for you to become a naturalist or wildlife preservationist, except for your entirely selfish individual experience, your intellectual-emotional experience. Any other argument, I believe, is spurious. By adhering to conventional (rational) arguments for wildlife preservation, and by continuing to obey conventional rules of argument, we illustrate the limitations of our own perception and of our own individual and collective experience.

CHAPTER FOUR
Experiencing

If, to this stage, this essay has appeared to be a deliberate attempt at vivisection, I suppose that perception would be justified. I have tried, as best I could, to strip away at least a few of the more obvious layers of rhetoric that surround the corpus of wildlife conservation arguments, and to de-mystify that rhetoric toward the revealing of what seem to me to be the essential issues. Of course when you set about unwinding the rhetorical cocoon from almost any concern, you run the risk of exposing false expectations for what they are, and of experiencing at least some measure of disappointment. Shocking to relate, it frequently appears in the final analysis that there was not very much there after all. This is not an appealing notion, but it does serve to remind us why the rhetoric was there in the first place.

The argument for wildlife conservation has been variously framed and in various species of rhetoric because it was felt necessary to present it in those forms in the absence of a cultural belief system that could accommodate wildlife preservation – in my terminology – for its own sake. That, in practice, would clearly be a preposterous argument. Ergo, suitable rationalizations had to be found, and some of these we have discussed. For reasons I have already outlined, I believe that these rationalizations are incapable of meeting the needs of wildlife. Our uniquely human self-deluding is practised even in endeavours such as this.

On the basis of some experience in conservation affairs, I am at last persuaded that mere argument as such is entirely worthless. Indeed, as I have tried to show, some of our arguments (certainly the most-used ones) may even be detrimental to our purpose in that they tend to reinforce the very belief system that gives rise to our problems in the first place (evidence, for example). Argument, it seems to me, is never going to help wildlife. It rarely has, and there is little to persuade me that it ever will, appreciably. If anything is going to help wildlife it is individual people. Not people in the mass; after all, the public is no more than a concept. The reality is an aggregate of individuals. I believe that wildlife preservation is entirely dependent upon *individual human experience*. Unashamedly, I shall now set about attempting to build a rhetorical environment for that belief.

I have insinuated the notion of "experience" at various points. Individuals such as myself, who for various reasons have been unusually fortunate in having enjoyed a wealth of experiences with wildlife in many parts of the world, eventually are forced to adopt a kind of self-protective defensiveness about those experiences. Who are you, someone will say, to recommend cutting down on the flow of tourists in Africa, in the Pacific Islands, in Indo-China, in South America, in the arctic? You've been there; you've seen it. It's all right for you to say these things. Yes, of course, I am supposed to say: *mea culpa*. Yes, I have been in all of these places and more, and yes, I say there are too many of me. What else can I possibly say? Yes, I recommend denying those experiences to you – in the interest of wildlife.

First of all, I am not in the least embarrassed by or apologetic for my good fortune and what may appear to be your lack of it. I shall attempt to show that all is available to you anyway. All of it. That is because the "nature" experience is entirely qualitative, not measurable, not rational. You will have to accept on faith my statement that nothing has been added to my qualitative experience since I was ten years old. There have been many quantitative overlays, many adventures, many data, many sights and sounds, and all the rest of it, but the quality has remained absolutely unchanged since my childhood. The initial experience was everything, and has continued in its original form life-long. Without it, subsequent adventures would have meant no more than those of any other tourist.

There was behind my parents' house a city ravine, with a little stream running through it. At one end, before the stream disappeared into a large pipe, there was a little marshy area where the water spilled shallowly to one side. There, there were toads and frogs and newts. If you lay very quietly in the grass at the water's edge, you could observe them. The longer you looked, the more deeply you were mesmerized... possessed. There was no world whatever, outside that world... nothing beyond shimmering light on water, smooth clean muck, green plants, trickling sounds, flickering tadpoles, living, *being*. That was when the pain started.

The knife of separation is cruel. I not only remember in a factual sense but I can *feel* to this day the anguished frustration, the knowledge that I could never–not ever–be more than a boy on the grass, excluded from that world wholly and eternally. But why? Why pick on me? I wished it no harm; I only wanted to be part, to join, to "plug in." The denial was impersonal and cold and final. It has gnawed at me ever since–not all the time, mercifully–but much of it.

I wept over it, in a dogwood thicket. In the certainty that through no apparent fault of my own I was being unjustly denied something that was as fundamentally important as air, I felt much anguish at times. Unpredictably, of course, as it is with pre-adolescents, there would be unexpected moments of pure and inexpressible joy and happiness when the "free flow" between nature and myself was unobstructed and open. Such moments always seemed to happen accidentally: why couldn't I *will* them? Always there was a mix of sadness and pleasure. My early experience with nature was bittersweet; it still is. I rejoice in wildlife and I despair, in equal measure.

That is one side of it. Plans were revealed for the construction of a storm sewer through "my" ravine. Shock, dismay, and all the rest of it were mine early. The ten-year-old mind is not subtle: how can I warn the frogs and toads and newts? Can I get them out of there, take them away somewhere? They are defenceless; it is wrong to hurt them. What right do we have to hurt them when we cannot warn them? They don't know what is happening, or why. There was much puzzlement here. All logic seemed to be backwards or upside-down; nothing made sense. I could do nothing but watch, with sorrow and fury.

But why the sorrow and the fury? What *is* compassion, after all, and where does it come from? And why do so many other people feel nothing at all? Those questions are as germane today as they were when I was ten. It seems clear now that, although there was no gainsaying the intensity of my emotion, my feeling for the wildlife beings involved, the sorrow and fury, were perhaps entirely on my own behalf. I was responding intensely because *I* was being impinged upon.

I think that through those moments of "free flow," in the grass by the pond beneath the dogwoods, the toads and the frogs and the newts and their hypnotic sunlight had been irreversibly incorporated into my world, literally into *me*. *My* world was being tampered with; *I* was being invaded. Next spring I would have a piece missing, chewed out of me by the ditch diggers. The hurt was much more than resentment and sympathy. It was real, and I would feel it always.

It can never be otherwise. You, the individual experiencer, are paramount, because the emotional investment is yours alone. There is but one universe and it is you. But the experience need not be immediate and on-site. Despite repeated attempts, and despite even having heard and smelled him, and having photographed his fresh footprint, I have never *seen* a wild tiger. At this late date – meaning both my own chronology and the status of the tiger population – I probably never will. That is not as important to me now as it used to be, because the fortunes of the tiger are no less close to me for that. The tiger is already an integral part of me, and his fate is mine. He entered me with the toads and frogs and newts. My experience is *my* experience and the physical proximity of the tiger really has rather little to do with it. I shall be just as depressed by bad news of the tiger, and just as elated by good news of him, as I would have been had we lived side by side. Wildlife preservation "for its own sake" is for the sake of the experiencer. Each experience, whether physical or intuitive, adds to my universe. Each extinction subtracts from it.

Now, this is not an argument of self-interest. Earlier in this essay I decried those arguments because I believe them to be inherently weak at best, dishonest and destructive at worst. Self-interest is just that: personal advantage, personal motive, personal gain, personal profit. That is not what wildlife preservation, in the "ideal" sense, is. Wildlife preservation for its own sake – for your sake – is none of these things, because it cannot be viewed comparatively and it cannot be measured. It is an experiential phenomenon only, and it cannot be "valued" (weighed). It happens singularly and uniquely and exclusively in your universe. Wildlife as part of your world, and part of you, and that is all that matters. That is what preservation is.

I have no doubt that it will be charged that this is not a reasonable argument. It is too "mystical," not sufficiently logical. I feel that the conventional arguments for conservation are unequal to the task, not because they are not rational (most of them try to be), but because *there is no rational argument for wildlife preservation*. There is no rational argument for personal, individual, qualitative experience. There can be no rational argument for your universe or for mine. They simply are – whatever they are. Neither you nor I need accept any obligation to rationalize those universes; indeed such exercises have a way of being severely self-defeating.

My point here is quite simple. Rationalizations are substitutes for qualitative (as opposed to abstract) experience. Once the experience has been incorporated into oneself, there is no need for either rationalization or proselytism. There is no "reason" for wildlife preservation. It is a state of being.

There was a time when sensible people knew that reason and experience could not be torn asunder; together, they were "knowledge." It is this knowledge of which I speak – the state of being that is wildlife preservation. Today, however, its two parts are conceptually polarized. We have rationality (science) and we have mysticism (non-rational experience). We have intellect as distinct from emotion. We have reason/feeling, and we have man/nature.

As indicated at the outset, I have complained long and widely about the intellect/emotion duality in the conservation context. Anyone with a shot glass of intelligence can follow most logical argument, but inevitably there appears some "block" that prevents the *emotional acceptance* of man as a biologic being, with all that that implies. We have forgotten that what makes the world go round is compliance, not logic.

The potentially fertile union of reason and non-rational experience is made impossible for wildlife conservation because there is no emotional impetus for that union, but (in our culture) much resistance to it. Remember that the "academic" problem is one in which there is little emotional investment in the solution but very much in the method. Wildlife preservation, as I understand it, is the antithesis of the academic problem.

At the root of our wildlife preservation difficulties are the perceived dichotomies that flow from the "mind/matter," "spirit/flesh" dualism inherent in western cosmologies. And not only are mind and spirit separate from matter and flesh, they are *superior* to them. Mind *over* matter, remember. So it is that man stands to non-man as intellect stands to emotion. Man/nature : intellect/emotion. There you have the fundamental and operational formula of the technocratic age and the failure of wildlife preservation in that age.

It seems to me that just as our culture teaches us to perceive a gap between intellect and emotion, at the same time we feel some "irrational" (inherent, natural) urge to seal over or close that gap. But we are prevented from doing so. Culture covers the institutionalized gap with an artificial membrane, a fabricated gloss of beliefs, givens, religions, philosophies, ideologies – rationalizations. Remember that rationalizations are substitutes for experience. For purposes of the scientific-technocratic juggernaut it is necessary for us to *perceive* a gap between intellect and emotion, but that gap must on no account be experienced in a qualitative sense. It would vanish forthwith–and then where would high civilization be? So it is covered over with a transparent plasticized veneer of assumptions so that it may be seen but not touched.

So it is with the necessary gap between man and nature. It must be maintained at any cost, for reasons I have already put forward. Unlike the gulf between intellect and emotion, however, it *must* be "experienced" (in pre-selected fragments) for its continued maintenance. Here the *illusion* of experience is provided through the same beliefs, givens, religions, philosophies, ideologies–the same panoply of rationalizations. Here again rationalization is substituted for the whole (idea + quality) experience, because of course the man/nature gap cannot be experienced. It doesn't exist. Man, after all, *is* nature.

The intellect/emotion gap must not be "experienced" because if it were, the experiencer would *know* (reason + experience) that it does not exist either. The ordered universe of the Rational Being would fly apart. In the final accounting–or the ideal knowledge–there is of course no abyss: man and nature are one, intellect and emotion are one. I experienced this–although I could not articulate it–at ten years of age. Both dichotomies are entirely conceptual and artificial. Both are purely symbolic.

As I have pointed out earlier, we have a nasty and persistent way of taking our symbols (metaphors, models) for absolutes–for truth. Thus we accept the "reality" of order and purpose, beginnings and ends, predictability and control, meaning and direction in the anthropocentric universe. Ideas, all of them. Rationalizations that cannot be corroborated by experience. In the classical sense at least, scarcely "knowledge."

Symbolic representations are used for many reasons, including as a kind of shorthand. Perversely, however, we tend to confuse our shorthand for the real thing. Thus "God" becomes infinitely more real than that which it represents; "species" becomes the reality as opposed to the process it symbolizes; "hour" is seen as concrete and tangible, no longer a conceptual unit of measurement. Usually, apart from such as mathematics and music, where the shorthand is a genuine tool, symbols turn out to be no more than metaphors for that which is inexpressible–most often for that which is not understandable or manageable. And, as often as not, symbols are used to metaphorically conceal root fears. The rationalization is substituted for the experience out of fear of the experience. Thus, when I was very young, flags and bands used to ennoble war. The vivisectionist never kills an animal; he sacrifices it. You never perform autopsies on people, only on bodies.

For me, the most interesting symbolic-metaphoric rationalization of all time is the uniquely human immortal soul. In my earlier discussion of the immortality imperative, I remained at the species level. There is no *individual* immortality imperative. We know better than that, on purely empirical grounds. So we invent a comfortable continuity called the afterlife, together with a vehicle for its achievement. No objective evidence can ever shatter this one; no contrary experience can ever be brought to bear. It is unspeakably gorgeous; of all the products of human ingenuity it is supreme, for it can never be disproven. Here, it seems to me, the institutionalized intellect/emotion dichotomy is revealed for what it is.

I now see the root fears at work in these issues somewhat differently than I once did. In western post-renaissance tradition there is a fundamental vested interest in the preservation of reason from the inroads of feeling (man/nature). The buffer between them is of cultural fabrication, a rational response to an irrational fear. So it is with individuals, well and truly conditioned as we are. The fundamental fear, I think now, is of disorganization–of emotion eroding the integrity of the conceptual (reasonable) edifice that, we believe, is each of us.

Remember the classic accusation that is levelled against wild-life preservationists. We are *emotional*. When confrontation with our opponents reaches the abusive stage–which it can do–the ultimate crushing charge, designed to wholly discredit us, is that we are emotional. Emotion is unmanageable, unclassifiable, unreasonable, untrustworthy. It is illogical. A terribly prominent and respectable elderly gentleman thus castigated me many years ago; flushed purple, sweating, trembling, he brought his elegantly manicured fist crashing to the table. "You naturalists are nothing but starry-eyed idealists–you're nothing but *emotional*!" he panted. That should have put me in my place for keeps.

I happen to loathe and abominate blood "sports." I think that killing any sensate being for recreation–for fun–is evil and contemptible. I have said so, for public consumption, many times. The most frequent theme in the resulting letters I receive is that I have absolutely no rational argument to present, and that as the result I (sneakily) resort to purely emotional appeals. Some of the mail, by the way, has to be opened with my asbestos gloves. I find this interesting.

In San Diego, California, there is an institution called "Sea World." This is a superb marine aquarium–probably the best I have ever seen–that is severely marred by a number of nauseatingly anthropomorphic captive dolphin, whale, and sea lion shows. (In these shows the animals' tricks and routines are without exception described as "behaviours" by the ringmasters. Either this is to bring a kind of clinical scientific aura to the performances or to intimate that the demeaning acts are "natural"; I am not sure.) In any event they are no whit different from the dressed-up chimp shows of my childhood or the hat-wearing cycling bears of the Moscow circus, which I find embarrassing and saddening. Yes, I *am* emotional. Aren't you?

At the San Diego "Sea World," last time I was there, there was prominently displayed the following message:

THE EXISTENCE OF ZOOS, OCEANARIUMS AND AQUARIUMS IS BEING THREATENED!

You and your children may not be able to have the thrilling experience of visiting a zoo or oceanarium much longer.

Harmful and restrictive legislation is threatening the continued existence of these institutions, long dedicated to the protection and conservation of animals.

Much of this legislation–hastily conceived, often poorly interpreted and rigidly enforced–has been proposed by influential, emotionally oriented, pressure groups.

Through a lack of information and cooperation, their good intentions have resulted in often harming the very animals they sought to protect.

ZOOACT, formed by members of the zoological community, can provide a way to halt this threatening trend–before it's too late.

There is much in this to analyze, including among other things the claim that such institutions contribute to the protection and conservation of animals–a claim I have never seen substantiated. I have already made some reference to that. Relevant at this stage in our discussion is the careful and deliberate injection of that dirty word again. Our emotional orientation, it would appear, comes close to being a crime against nature.

What is this pejorative use of the word "emotion" really all about? Even the most casual investigation seems to show that emotions evoke fear. I think it is fear of the chaotic. To be emotional means to set aside organization (reason) and to drift perilously toward chaos – or at least to allow it to intrude sufficiently to threaten the edifice of reason. Like many others, the conservationist fears personal and wider disorder; like many others, he values his reasonable universe. Naturally, our opponents appeal to the public emotion in order to condemn our emotion, turning disadvantage into instant advantage. In so doing, they respond to and project their own worst fears – with human emotion.

Since emotions cannot be explained rationally, the wildlife preservationist is once again saddled with an impossible burden of proof. We don't even know what emotions *are* – merely that they exist. But that existence can only be shown within an experiential context – never by rational explication. There is no such thing as an emotion in isolation; it must have a context. You have to love or fear or hate *something* – even if it is only yourself. Unfortunately for all of us, the technocratic-scientific bowdlerization of "reason + experience = knowledge" into "reason + rationalization = knowledge" ensures that the experiential evidence, soft though it may well be, cannot be admitted.

Here is what I have referred to as our "double-bind." In the desperate attempt to show at any cost that we are not emotional, that we are entirely reasonable, we mount such incredibly twisted "rational" arguments as some of those reviewed earlier. We accept the onus of projecting and sharing that strange world view which is our own most intransigent difficulty. Wildlife preservation is for emotional, intuitive, irrational folk – women, for example. And so it goes. Every challenge we attempt to meet on its terms, rather than on our own grounds, creates new and even more recalcitrant problems. Our fear of appearing to be emotional requires us to fabricate our own rationalizations lest we invite the terrible censure of the technocratic age by committing its one unpardonable sin – irrationality.

If, as I suspect it to be, the root fear is of disorganization, then appropriate vigilance must be maintained for the general security. The conceptual edifice of rationality, in spite of itself, *knows* (reason + experience) that it is vulnerable, and acts accordingly. Thus we have orthodoxies and the threats of reprisal that protect them. If there is no split between man and nature, then man is no more than an animal – and you know what *that* means. It means, among other things, no human uniqueness in the matter of immortal souls. And that means total disorganization of the edifice, for keeps. Close ranks, brethren, your self-interest is on the line.

The only alternative to closing ranks is to open the kingdom to all comers. There is some precedent for this; women can vote now, in some places. In the time frame of human history, it was only an eyelash-blink ago that Europeans were justified in putting to the torch creatures that *looked* human but obviously were not because they had never heard of Jesus Christ. Even more recently it required a monstrous bloodbath to determine that one man has no right to own another. Eventually, however, even women, Indians, and blacks have been accepted into the human species and granted some but not all of the perquisites of membership.

It has been pointed out that the fearful atrocities of earlier times and of our own day are made possible in large measure by a conceptual-perceptual trick known as "pseudo-speciation." You don't napalm people; you napalm gooks. Thus we have wogs and niggers and spics and kykes and all the rest of it. Such are the uses of symbolism. The murderer on the loose or in the dock is an "animal"; social ideals and ethics no longer apply. Pseudo-speciation frees us from rules against killing, cruelty, and other uncivilized "animal" behaviour. Man/nature.

It may very well be that the rational fear of emotion is more intimately related to the human fear of nature than we like to think. Clearly the Rational Being occupies his place on the power pyramid because it is in the universal nature of things that reason is more important than non-reason and thus that man is more important than non-man. (This of course is a classic after-the-fact rationalization; it would not have been made in australopithecine times.) The fear of disorganization of the power structure is as profound as the fear of personal disorganization – perhaps even more so.

Fear of disorganization (breakdown) is fear of the loss of control. The applicability of this in the individual emotional sense needs no further emphasis. I would suggest, however, that the identical fear sustains the conceptual man/nature dichotomy. That which is not under control is threatening, whether it be the backyard crabgrass, the spruce budworm, the source of crude oil, the stock market, or oneself. An acquaintance of mine in the arctic town of Inuvik once said to me, "John, we've got to do something about all these ravens here in town!" "Why so?" I asked. "For heaven's sake, man, look around you—there are so *many* of them! They're going to be out of *control!*"

Loss of control is the abdication of power. It is tantamount to chaos. The universe is orderly, therefore chaos is unnatural. The universe operates according to ultimate laws, therefore chaos is immoral. That which cannot be controlled (managed, manipulated) may be seen as both unnatural and immoral—psychopathic. The unmanageable is that "animal" side of us that surfaces in criminal court from time to time. The unmanageable is also the mountain peaks and the ocean abyss and the farthest ice-packs and the rain and the drought and all other such items as have not yet been boxed into the management chart of the human organization. So it is seen that the ravens of Inuvik (prospering on our garbage) are thumbing their amiable beaks at universal order and thus at us.

We resent and fear disorder, the absence of control, the breakdown of authority, the weakening of predictability. I believe that the individual fear of death is also the fear of disorganization. It is culturally conditioned, and it works. As we have seen, there is no individual immortality imperative, only a species one. Where our culture sees to it that the species immortality imperative is kept solidly in place, and it can do nothing about individual mortality, it does maintain a deep and abiding *fear* of mortality in the individual. Fear of the *experience* of death is not innate in us; it is created and sustained entirely culturally, which means rationally. Death is the final sting, the ultimate victory of uncontrollable, unmanageable, immoral, chaotic *nature*—from which experience we are snatched at the final exhalation by the gorgeous rationalization. Spirit over flesh, man over nature.

No example of the role of rationalization in sustaining the man/nature and reason/emotion polarities can compete with this one. It is the conclusive denial of the role of experience in knowledge. It is the conclusive act of closure. It is the final and absolute rejection of human membership in life process, the last unilateral decree of divorce from sentient Earth, the transcendent taxonomy. No longer do we have the jesuitical life kingdoms of plants, animals, man; now we are back to two, but a different two—biotic being, and man. The apogee in dualism is the perigee in self-delusion.

The belief system is quite unable to accommodate the experiential content of the classic knowledge equation. Such experiences as emotion and feeling are admitted into the model of reality only where to deny flatly their existence would be palpably irrational, as for example in dreaming or other common experience.

If, as I believe them to be, rationalizations are short-term "hypes" that are injected into the vacuum of empty experience, then all the wildlife conservation arguments in the world that are mounted from a would-be "rational" base are predestined for failure. If wildlife preservation really *is* for its own sake—which means for the experiencer's sake—then there can never be any "reason" for it. There is no rational argument for experiencing; it is above and beyond all logical capture.

The experiential vacuum is not part of our biology. It is entirely a matter of cultural conditioning, of nurture. There is no limit to experience in us, so far as I can detect, save what we cold-bloodedly and self-consciously impose upon ourselves in response to the conceptual tyranny of western "civilization." All is not lost, however. Once we recognize that there really *are* cultural (purely artificial) barriers to our experience, it is possible to begin to entertain the possibility of breaching them. Our minds *can* be opened to qualities of experience that will eventually allow us the state of being that is wildlife preservation. Only one act is required, and that is perhaps the most difficult (and yet, paradoxically, the easiest) you have ever undertaken. That is the act of opening.

Opening is a tricky business, and as in any other act of compliance, it gets more difficult if you allow yourself to brood about it. As the churchmen well know, you never can tell what might fly in. I think of the cultural belief system as a great white soft swollen belly. Incise it, and much will tumble out. The root dread, however, is of contamination that might *enter*. This dread pervades all of our institutions. It is why ecology has sometimes been called the "subversive science." Now, many a proselytizer will urge you to "open up"; he means, of course, just enough to allow the insertion of his particular offering, against which the hope is that you will have no antibodies.

To open is to make yourself consciously and deliberately vulnerable. It is an act of acceptance, an act of compliance. Opening may take a modicum of courage, but so did your very first public speech, your first dive off the high board, your first driving lesson, your first parachute jump, your first acceptance of mortality, your first serious doubt.

Opening is conscious and deliberate compliance with what *is*, not with what is imagined. It is the acceptance of whatever comes, the discarding of comparative "values," the denial of no possibilities, the entertaining of all possible impressions. Thus experience of wild nature becomes experience of our selves. It is no longer the perception (imaging, matching, rationalizing, identifying) of the world, but of *being* it. This is no mere empathizing; it is experiencing.

CHAPTER FIVE

The State of Being

The other morning—just a day or two before this page went into my typewriter—I was awakened smartly at dawn by the close whooping morning song of a troop of gibbons. Rushing out the door, I very nearly fell over an unfamiliar blonde five-year-old in spectacles and blue pyjamas, sitting elbows on knees, chin cupped in hands, unmoving, intent. She glanced up somewhat sternly, as though to shush me, and softly whispered "Monkeys." I was rude enough to ask whether she could see the apes (I wanted to). She shook her head, wiping me from her world wholly and finally. At last I had the grace to sit and listen too.

The jungle shrieked and shook and crescendoed and echoed and re-echoed, and a mynah bird picked up the theme. I have heard many a dawn chorus in many a place, but I shall never forget that one, that quality. The overwhelming primate celebratory songs, the green dripping rain forest, the faint glowing early light, the intense little kid, the toads and the frogs and the newts, and—once again—free flow.

When I was very young the experience was entirely accidental, unpredictable, ungovernable. It came and it went, and much of the anguish in the awareness of separation was caused by one's lack of control of free flow. You couldn't hold it, and you couldn't command it. It just happened—and then it was gone. A frequent fear was that it might be gone for good; but it never was. It is still here, still alive and well, and thanks to some non-rational, experiential, unreasonable, acultural, non-intellectual, emotional contrivance that defies all logic, in the right circumstances may now be summoned almost at will.

A day or two before the gibbons and blue pyjamas episode I found myself at 2.30 in the morning on a vast moonlit beach watching a seven-foot-long leatherback sea turtle dig a deep pit in the loose sand, lay forty-two eggs in it, cover the nest, and laboriously make her way back into the shimmering South China Sea. Since I was watching in the usual schizoid way of the naturalist, marvelling at it all whilst at the same time paying keen attention to each minute detail and considering the chances of hatching success, hatchling survival, turnover, and all the rest of it, it was prudent to hold the free flow for later.

That moment came when the great reptile finally heaved her immense bulk to meet the first wavelet at the shore. A dancing splash wiped the grainy sand from one enormous eye. A shuddering abyssal breath, another ponderous lurch, and her foreflippers were in the water. The slope is gradual here, and the turtle was still treading sand for more than twenty yards. But the heaves became easier, more rapid, more fluid, and at last she floated.

She remained on the surface for several moments, possibly to catch her breath. In those moments, as gentle ripples broke soundlessly over the gigantic carapace, now wetly silver in the moonlight, my universe was no longer mine alone. It was ours. With the leatherback turtle, I slipped beneath the smooth surface of the sea... As the ceaseless cycle turns, universe without end, life without beginning, pulse without destiny, form without function, love without self, circling among unknown stars, we are once again *in touch*.

I do not know how long I stood there in the shallows, but when I again perceived the ocean in a "waking" way the turtle was long gone. I was quite alone. The group of which I was part had moved a little distance down the beach to watch another leatherback going through the same ancient procedures. Though I too watched the second one, there was really no need to, and I knew it. All had been accomplished and incorporated – finally and forever – already.

Now, my point in reporting all of this is not to apply one more layer of mystery (mysticism) to the wildlife experience, but rather to emphasize that when I say that the fate of the sea turtle or the tiger or the gibbon is mine, I mean it. All that is in my universe is not merely mine; it is *me*. And I shall defend myself.

I shall defend myself not only against overt aggression, but also against gratuitous insult. There is a splendidly designed polar bear exhibit at the Metropolitan Toronto Zoo, on the outside wall of which is a plaque announcing that the exhibit was made possible by Imperial Oil Limited. I have mentioned already that my archetype of the ugly, offensive, and disgusting is the 45-gallon fuel drum. Since Imperial Oil Limited is one of the prime "developers" of the Canadian arctic, I interpret the tastelessness of this particular exercise in the context of the claims of zoos with respect to the protection and conservation of animals.

All, however, is not gibbons, leatherback turtles, and polar bears. For most of us, these are "exotics." They are important, but they are not everything. No individual species or group of species is everything. As I have tried to point out, the limits of "everything" turn out to be the limits of individual internalized experience. And the potential for this is limitless. Free flow is available to you anywhere – if you allow it.

Domestic animals are not part of my operational definition of "wildlife," but they are sensate beings, and many pets are willing to accept you into their states of being if you behave circumspectly and appropriately. This can be greatly helpful as a beginning. For a long time I and a number of others loved a tough old tomcat who with muscle and know-how ruled absolutely and for a surprising number of years several blocks in old residential Toronto. Also, surprising for a tomcat, he died not of wounds and injuries but of sheer age. He was aloof and self-contained, and he knew all there was to know, but he was tolerant of humans. Rarely, he would allow communication at the level of which I speak. One example will do. Very late one night, I was occupying one kitchen stool, he another. Everyone else was asleep. Suddenly, out of long, long silence, he stirred and *spoke* to me. What he said was brief and not susceptible to translation, but something prompted me to put my head to his, to open, to listen, and to accept. Something prompted me to *comply* – to my everlasting profit. For now the scarred and tattered and lumpy old puss and I can resume our free flowing circuitry whenever either of us wishes.

There is absolutely nothing unusual about this experience. Anyone who has ever loved a nonhuman being knows the extraordinarily encompassing sense of unity that is possible, at least occasionally. I am certain that you know the feeling as well as I do. I suggest, however, that rather than an end in itself this experience is merely the beginning – the opening of a gate that leads to the very nature of being, the nature of life experience and of life preservation. All I ask here is that you allow yourself to extend this selfless "identification" – for that, essentially, is what it is – beyond those individual beings that you "know" in the conventional sense. Touch is good, but not essential. The animal need never know of your presence, for the bond is ancient and indestructible, and *you* are playing the active role in opening your world to his. So long as you are able to crack the plastic cultural

capsule sufficiently to allow *his* universe to flow into yours, you
have begun to grow. Put your head to the head of the tomcat; the
tiger is near. The final step is accomplished when you can find
(retrieve) the tiger in your universe at will, and the tomcat is no
longer required as facilitator. Let him sleep; you know now what
his dreams are made of.

Steal one moment away from your striving, and look at the
cock pigeon strutting on the eavestrough. Look at him; *see* him.
That wildly staring ruby eye looks a bit crazy, and it would be if it
were in your head, but it's in that pigeon head; it belongs.
Absorbed as he is in his display ritual, he may slightly lose his
balance, career for an instant in an undignified way, then regain
his composure. It looks funny, but he doesn't fall. You would be
killed. See the bird; really *see* him, and *feel* the urgency and the
perfection and the beauty of his hot being. Forget your self-
consciousness and your stereotypes; set aside your image-cards
and accept what is right in front of you. Know that you and he
pulse as one, and that you always did. You may not look the
same, but you and the pigeon are no more than differently assem-
bled manifestations of one thing, one process, one being. *Experience* that state of being, passively. Recall that state of being the
next time you hear of someone poisoning pigeons. You too will
be sick at your stomach.

In Vera Cruz you can buy a rock band consisting of stuffed
bullfrogs, each holding a tiny instrument. In Nairobi you can buy
an umbrella stand made from the foot of an elephant and a fly-
whisk made from a zebra's tail. In Bangkok you can buy a stuffed
mongoose and a stuffed cobra, locked in eternal embrace. In
Puerto Vallarta you can buy two stuffed pond turtles dancing a
fandango. In T'aipei you can buy chessmen and ear-rings carved
from elephants' tusks. In Hong Kong you can buy an aphrodisiac
made from powdered rhinoceros horn. In Kuala Lumpur you can
buy a jungle butterfly embedded in plastic on a key chain. In
Frobisher Bay you can buy a narwhal tusk. In Caracas you can
buy a shrunken monkey head.

In the alchemist's dungeon that is almost any well-appointed
shopping centre in the "developed" world, you can buy cosmetics, transmission fluid, and pet food made from whales; you
can buy the hide of a lynx in the form of a hat, or gloves made
from the skin of an unborn lamb; you can buy a coat made from
seal whelps; you can buy a tropical finch in a metal cage and a
Siamese fighting fish in a plastic bag; you can buy firearms and
whammo ammunition, and multiple hooks with barbs on them;

you can buy sharkskin shoes and the unspawned eggs of a sturgeon; you can buy the pulverized enlarged liver of a force-fed goose and the testicles of a bull and the brain of a calf; you can buy chemical biocides and plant growth inhibitors; you can buy the sterile eggs of an untrod chicken and the tongue of a feed-lot steer that spent its last weeks hock-deep in its own manure; you can buy medicines made from the blood and viscera of living laboratory animals.

You can also buy the Holy Bible and the Declaration of Human Rights.

As every wildlife preservationist knows to his cost, the simple minded among us are wont to interpret our anger as misanthropy. I try to tell them that we are honest folk; if we were misanthropists, we would say so. Still, it is often charged that we "care more for animals than for people"—again an unwitting emphasis of the "man/nature" problem. This, as I perceive it, is cultural constipation at its fullest. It is impossible for such as these to shift—even momentarily—outside the cultural hallucination sufficiently to see that what we care about is life—all life in all forms—or, perhaps better expressed, living. I care for the phenomenon of living more than I care for the contorted belief system of my culture. I care for wildlife preservation more than I care for its opposite—the technomachine and that which serves it. I care most deeply of all about the failure of wildlife preservation in my lifetime.

At the outset I hypothesized that those arguments we have mounted for wildlife preservation have been unequal to the task. Initially, my faith in that hypothesis was grounded simply enough in the widespread accelerating decline and disappearance of wildlife and wild places. At least on that evidence our arguments seemed insufficient. So they were put to the test; we looked at the most prevalent groups and families of arguments in order to try to see what it was about them that made them so apparently ineffective. This led us to certain underlying (root) problems that appeared to become even more important than the mere inadequacy of our stated case. Indeed they seemed to militate against *any* kind of argument. Argument might not be a factor after all.

In other words, the opening hypothesis seemed to have been correct, but for reasons other than my original ones. Most of my starting assumptions have been revealed for what they were—unfounded assumptions. We have seen that there can be no "rational" argument for wildlife preservation, just as there can be no logical explanation of quality experience. It now seems to me that argument *itself*–in the sense of reasonable dialogue–is not only inappropriate to our subject matter but also may be destructive of it. There is no "logic" in feeling, in experiencing, in states of being. Yet, these same phenomena appear to be pre-requisite for wildlife preservation.

One of the more peculiar traits of our society is its assumption–its insistence–on solutions. Just as there are reasons for all things, so there are solutions for all things. Always there are ultimate answers; there is no problem that is not amenable to logical reduction. This, as we have seen earlier, in spite of such bewildering enterprises as ecology. I have no "solution" to the wildlife preservation problem. There may not be one. But given the somewhat shaky assumption that one exists, I sense that I can at least feel the direction.

The direction seems to lie in the compliant acceptance by individual human beings of membership–which is to say, "place"–in the beauty that is life process. This is too easy for me to say, for the difficulties are formidable. Such an act–a conscious and willing act of self-recovery–would require the re-cognition of options that have long been masked from us by our accumulated tradition. It would require the healing of perceived dichotomies, the mending of conceived alienations, the redirection of our fabricated imperatives toward reconciliation with that long-forgotten quality that is the nature of being. It would be the dissolution of the ancient western divorce from nature.

Throughout this essay I have called attention to the many symptoms of our malaise–our discontent, our uneasy rationalizations, our gnawing ambitions, our terrible paranoia–with respect to our perceived purpose in the scope of things. I interpret these and other symptoms as illustrating the frustration of a fundamental biological (and thus human) drive toward wholeness, toward belonging. Implacably and relentlessly, our culture keeps us blinded to the qualitative sensory options that are ever at hand and infinite in number.

The fallacy that is conventional wildlife conservation is a flat denial of those options. I cannot know whether your or my qualitative experience of nature will ever benefit wildlife, but I do know that the joy of self-recovery and liberation from cultural tyranny is contagious.